Motorcycle Journeys Through

Texas

by Neal Davis

Whitehorse Press
Center Conway, New Hampshire

Whitehorse Press books are also available at
discounts in bulk quantity for sales and promotional
use. For details about special sales or for a catalog of
motorcycling books and videos, write to the
publisher:
   Whitehorse Press
   107 East Conway Road
   Center Conway, New Hampshire 03813-4012
   Phone: 603-356-6556 or 800-531-1133
   E-mail: CustomerService@WhitehorsePress.com
   Internet: www.WhitehorsePress.com

ISBN-13: 978-1-884313-44-8
ISBN-10: 1-884313-44-2

10 9 8 7 6 5 4 3

Printed in the United States of America

Dedication

This book is dedicated to the wonderful people of Texas. Getting to know these people and their attitudes while researching this book was a true delight. I hope they never change.

Other Touring Guides in
The Motorcycle Journeys Series

Motorcycle Journeys Through The Alps and Corsica

Motorcycle Journeys Through The Appalachians

Motorcycle Journeys Through Baja

Motorcycle Journeys Through California

Motorcycle Vagabonding In Japan

Motorcycle Journeys Through Northern Mexico

Motorcycle Journeys Through Southern Mexico

Motorcycle Journeys Through The Southwest

Also from Whitehorse Press

Motorcycle Touring and Travel:
A Handbook of Travel by Motorcycle

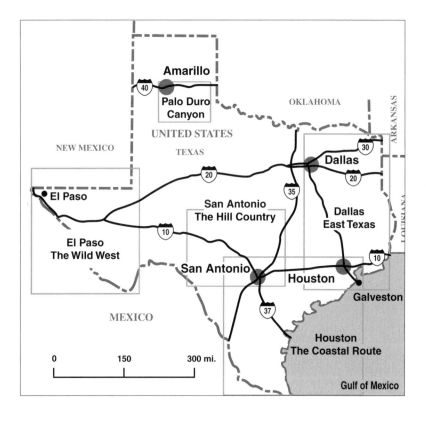

Contents

Dedication · 3

Acknowledgments · 7

Welcome to Texas · 9

A Proud History · 19

El Paso The Wild West · 27

El Paso to Fort Davis 34

Fort Davis to Presidio 38

Presidio to Big Bend National Park. 44

Exploring the River Roads 52

Big Bend to Marfa. 56

Marfa to Whites City, New Mexico 62

Whites City of El Paso via Cloudcroft, New Mexico. . . . 64

San Antonio The Hill Country · 69

San Antonio to Fredericksburg. 74

Fredericksburg to Austin (NE Loop) 80

Fredericksburg to Mason (NW Loop) 86

Fredericksburg to Luckenbach (SW Loop) 92

Fredericksburg to New Braunsfels (SE Loop) 98

Fredericksburg to Y.O. Ranch (W Loop) 106

Fredericksburg to San Antonio 110

Day Loop From San Antonio 112

San Antonio to Rocksprings 116

Rocksprings to Caverns (NW Loop) 120

Rocksprings to Camp Wood (SE Loop) 124

Rocksprings to Alamo Village (SW Loop) 128

Rocksprings to San Antonio 130

Houston The Coastal Route · 133

Houston to Galveston 136

Galveston to Rockport 142

Rockport to Port Isabel. 150

Port Isabel to Laredo 156

Laredo to Goliad 166

Goliad to Houston 172

Dallas-Fort Worth East Texas · 177

Dallas to Crockett 182

Crockett to College Station. 186

College Station to Galveston 192

Galveston to Jasper 198

Jasper to Jefferson or Shreveport. 204

Shreveport or Jefferson to Dallas 208

Palo Duro Canyon · 211

Motorcycle Transport · 214

Motorcycle Rentals · 216

San Antonio 216

Beaumont 217

El Paso 217

Houston 217

Austin 218

Dallas 218

Additional Resources · 219

About the Author · 224

Acknowledgments

Thanks to the wonderful staff at Whitehorse Press for their support and encouragement in preparing this book, without you guys and gals the project would have never have been completed. Skip Mascorro of Pancho Villa Mototours spent many hours marking maps, sharing secrets, and riding with me. His help is greatly appreciated. Also, thanks to the many people at the motorcycle dealerships throughout the state who took the time to help me find those special rides. A special thanks to Carol Smith for her input on the Rocksprings loops in the Hill Country chapter. Finally, thanks to all the other riders I met on the side of the road or over coffee who shared their personal experiences and favorite rides.

➡ Just How Big is Texas?

Everyone knows Texas is big. But how can we put this size in perspective? The following facts may help:

1) With a land area in excess of 267,000 square miles, Texas makes up more than 7 percent of the entire land mass of the United States. At its widest points, Texas is 801 miles from north to south and 773 miles from east to west. When it was accepted into the Union, Texas was given the option of subdividing into five smaller states.

2) Texas is larger than any European country, and larger than Germany, the United Kingdom, Ireland, Belgium, and the Netherlands *combined*.

3) Texas is larger than all the New England states, New York, Pennsylvania, Ohio and Illinois *combined*. Forty-one counties in Texas are each larger than the state of Rhode Island.

4) If you stand in the city of Orange on the east, you are closer to the Atlantic port of Savannah, Georgia, than you are to El Paso in the west. Of course you have to cross the states of Louisiana, Mississippi, Alabama, and Georgia to reach the Atlantic Ocean.

5) When standing in El Paso you are nearer to Los Angles than to Orange. Of course, you must pass through the states of New Mexico, Arizona, and California to reach the Pacific Ocean.

6) When you are in Brownsville in south Texas, you are closer to Mexico City than you are to the northern border of Texas and Oklahoma.

7) Standing at the northern border of Texas with Oklahoma, you can almost reach Canada before Brownsville in the south.

8) The Dallas-Fort Worth airport is larger than Manhattan Island.

Welcome to Texas

Everyone "knows" that Texas is just a huge, flat state. As one uninitiated friend said, "Texas is just a place to get across." While it is true that the vastness of Texas includes long, boring stretches; it also contains some of the best motorcycling roads in the world. Sure Texas is flat—if you leave out the almost 100 mountains that exceed 5,000 feet in altitude. Eight of which exceed 8,000 feet and God only knows how many sub-5,000-foot peaks. Sure, Texas is dry—if you exclude the more than 3 million acres of inland lakes and rivers, its 600 miles of oceanfront, and the countless bayous and swamps that cover the eastern part of the state. Sure, Texas has no trees—if you wish to ignore over 20 million acres of woodlands and the Big Thicket. The pur-

When pulling over to the side of the road for a break, always keep a sharp eye out for these "natives," as they are found throughout Texas in great numbers. (photo by Jack Lewis/TxDOT)

pose of this book is to introduce you to these areas with rides that are every motorcyclist's dream.

What is your riding preference? Do you want hills and twisties to test your sport-bike skills? If so, ride the Hill Country in central Texas or the piney woods in the east. Or, do you enjoy open spaces, dual-sport opportunities, and clear, starry nights? Then give west Texas a try, an area that includes the Davis and Franklin mountains. A visit to the Big Bend National Park will leave you wondering just how big the world must be. If you enjoy riding along mile after mile of pristine beaches with the ocean in view, check out the east coast. The southern route takes you through some wonderful areas to view wildlife, as well as many sites important in the history of the Republic of Texas. I hope you will ride the area that most appeals to you and return time after time to explore other routes. For those of you who live in Texas and have not explored other parts of the state, I hope this will encourage you to do so.

Not only is there superb riding in Texas, the culture and personality of the Lone Star State can be as unique and special as any exotic destination in the world. Some of the nation's largest cities are in Texas. Other sections have the lowest population density in the United States. The state was settled over a long period of time and its current inhabitants reflect both the myriad environmental differences and the diverse cultural backgrounds of original settlers.

In east Texas, you will find the French and Cajun influence evident in the architecture, food, pace of life, and speech patterns. Along the border with Mexico, a predominately Hispanic population commonly uses Spanish for roadside signs and daily interaction. The Hill Country hangs on to the food and language of its Germanic roots; at many area events, German is the most common tongue. West Texas leans heavily on its ranching and cowboy history.

Coming from such varied backgrounds, what binds these people into one called Texan? Texas was settled notably later than most other parts of the United States, by a sturdy stock of pioneers who tended to take risks and be somewhat less likely to bend to convention and authority. The image of Texas as projected by Hollywood tends to attract people of similar nature. Most who come here fall in love with it and become "naturalized" citizens. A female executive from the northeast who has never been on a horse in her life will soon own a pair of cowboy boots and hat for weekend social occasions. An "import" that has only been in the state a year or two will affect a certain swagger in his walk and talk. A popular bumper sticker sums up the attitude: "I was not born in Texas, but I got here as soon as I could."

Members of the Texas Sport Bike Association gather almost every weekend for a ride in the Hill Country.

It has been said that you cannot enter into any lengthy conversation with an ex-marine or Texan without soon being advised of that fact. Texans take a fierce pride in their state and its image. Any disparaging remark regarding the state will be met with at least a hostile glare—if not with some more active form of defense. Texans love to brag about their state and with some good reason. As Joe Namath once said, "If you can do it, it is not brag, but fact." Despite the ready defense of their home turf, Texans (named after the hospitable Tejas Indians) will go to great lengths to project their friendliness. They are, by and large, demonstrably nice folks.

Certain widely held perceptions about Texans are simply not true. I would guess that for every 10,000 people you see wearing cowboy outfits, only one will be a genuine cowboy. Not every Texan owns a pickup truck, although the state does lead the nation in truck registrations (California is a distant second). Not every Texan carries a gun; and although the percentage of people who do so is higher in Texas than in other parts of the country, they still represent a minority.

While Texas certainly contains its share of both good ol' boys and rednecks (God bless them), most Texans fit neither definition. Many will, however, make every effort to make you believe that they do. While the oil industry is still very important to the state, not all Texans are millionaires or

Bar-B-Q cook-offs are big events throughout Texas, with lots of ego and pride at stake. (photo by Michael A. Murphy/TxDOT)

owners of oil wells. And while Midland has the highest number of per capita millionaires in the country, the vast majority of the people in Texas reflect the general population of the nation in economic success.

It may be because of this diversity that you will find ready acceptance into almost all segments of Texas society. People are generally given a hearty welcome whatever their race, creed, or national origin and are accepted until they prove themselves deserving of less. Where else but Texas will you find a country music band called, "Kinky Friedman and His Texas Jew Boys" performing to enthusiastic dance hall audiences made up primarily of rednecks?

John Steinbeck wrote, "Texas is a state of mind, Texas is an obsession. Above all, Texas is a nation in every sense of the word."

Using this Book

Each chapter in this book is based from a major city with good air transportation services. You can ship your bike to that city, fly in, and be on your way, or you can arrange to rent a motorcycle when you arrive (see Appendix A2). I include a quick overview of each of these urban areas, but don't attempt to provide detailed sightseeing options in the major cities, because this book focuses on riding the open road. However, if you wish to spend a day or two exploring El Paso, San Antonio, Dallas, or Houston, there are many good guidebooks which cover the local sights. By spending some time exploring the major cities, you will get a better overall feeling and understanding for the variety of lifestyles in Texas. Along the roads, I have tried to point out interesting stops, side trips, eating places, and motorcycling hangouts.

How many miles make for a good day's ride? This varies widely with the rider and his or her style and habits. Think of days in hours instead of miles; the days in this book vary from less than one hundred miles (a lot of traffic and sightseeing) to almost four hundred (across wide open spaces of west Texas). The daily routes are planned so that your actual time from leaving your motel or campsite in the morning to arriving at your evening's destination will be eight to ten hours, including time for a short break mid-morning and mid-afternoon, a reasonable lunch stop, and occasional time off the bike

Texas state parks offer many superb locations to pitch a tent at very reasonable prices.

to stretch your legs and enjoy the roadside sights. Consider your own riding habits and adjust your plans as needed.

The daily routes suggested in this book are not direct routes from Point A to Point B. They try to get you onto the small backroads that are more enjoyable rides. As a result of this, you will encounter some turns where the signs indicate your next destination is in another direction. Follow the directions in the text, and you will eventually get to that destination too—but in a more interesting, fun way. Also, please consider all miles as approximations. Motorcycle odometers vary greatly and yours may not read exactly the same as the one used while riding the routes for this book.

In the major cities you will have the option of hotels and motels in every price range and category. Unless there is a truly unique place to stay, in or near these cities, this book does not make a recommendation. On the road, overnight stops have been chosen to be clean and generally moderately priced, with good dining facilities nearby. Sometimes you will have no other choice available. Where there is something noteworthy, I may point out ranches and resorts that are expensive. This book also suggests camping options, when available.

Texas offers all the usual fast food outlets in almost every town. I attempt to help you avoid these by pointing out local eateries that reflect the tastes of the area. Obviously, Bar-B-Q and Texas chicken-fried steak can be found almost everywhere. Tex-Mex cafés throughout the state offer some of the best

Along most Texas roads, you may encounter strange wildlife at any time. (photo by Gay Shackelford/TxDOT)

➡ High School Football

Texans have great pride and are fiercely competitive. Nowhere is this more evident than at a high school football game. Not only will the worth and reputation of the school be on the line, but the entire town's as well. It is not unusual for a promising prospect from far across the state to find that his parents are moving to a new job located in a town that just happens to need a player at his position. In larger cities, you will find 20,000-seat stadiums filled on Friday nights with screaming fans. When teams from smaller towns are playing on a rival's home turf, the entire town shuts down to travel with the team.

The game itself provides the purpose for the gathering, but the supporting casts of cheerleaders, flag corps, and bands make for a true extravaganza. The football coach is often the highest paid member of the faculty and typically has a staff of assistants and trainers to help him. Once, when a new professional player from Texas was asked how he was able to become a starter so quickly, he explained, "It was easy, the playbook up here is a lot simpler than what I used in high school."

Sadly, at many schools, education can take a back seat to football. In the mid-1980s, Texas school officials attempted to implement minimal academic standards for student athletes. This proposal was met with outrage throughout the state and was quickly rescinded, to be replaced by a "no pass, no play" rule that requires a three game suspension of any student failing a course. Of course, only a teacher with great courage and job security would ever consider failing a star player. ★

food anywhere in the world. The fresh seafood found along the coast is a delight. Certain rural sections of the state have culinary traditions you might not expect—German food in the Hill Country and Cajun cuisine in the east—but you should take advantage of the opportunity to enjoy these local specialties.

Planning a Trip

Texas is hot. During the months of July and August, riding a motorcycle can be less than enjoyable—even dangerous—due to the heat. Be careful to stay hydrated during warmer weather. The winter months can be wonderful, as long as you don't catch one of the few "blue northers" that come through two or three times a year. Fortunately, these cold snaps typically last only for a day or two. The best months in which to visit Texas include March through June and October through December. Along the coast and in the Hill Country, riding is a year-round sport.

➡ Just How Hot is a Texas Summer?

There are many sayings about how hot it gets in Texas during the summer. Here are a few:

1) Hot water comes from both taps.

2) The temperature drops below 90 degrees and you start looking for a sweater.

3) One of your biggest fears is that you will drop your bike in a parking lot and cook to death.

4) You realize that asphalt has a liquid state.

5) You coat your tongue with Tabasco sauce to cool your mouth off.

6) You realize the best parking spot is not the one nearest your destination, but where there is shade.   ✪

West Texas is dry, averaging less than eight inches of rain per year. East Texas, however, is quite wet, with up to fifty inches of rain per year (mostly in the summer months in the form of afternoon thundershowers or "frog stranglers").

If you enjoy attending motorcycle rallies and events, a wonderful free service is available through the people at Texmoto (www.texmoto.com), avid bikers and publishers of *Ride Texas* magazine. Once you have signed up for their free service, you will receive a weekly email listing events for the following month, including dates, locations, and links to the organizers' web sites.

Road Hazards and Driving Etiquette

Because of the heat, you should make sure you have a "foot" of some kind to place under your kickstand. Some people might not believe asphalt can exist in a liquid state. Those folks have never been to Texas during the summer! Roads in Texas are often resurfaced using the "chip and seal" method, a process whereby liquid asphalt is pored on an existing highway and then loose gravel is layered on top. After a few months, when the traffic has driven the gravel into the asphalt, the remaining gravel is removed. These areas are usually clearly marked by signs indicating loose gravel. Unless you happen upon one of these sections just a few days after the work was completed, they should present no real problem.

On routes that go through open-range country, livestock being in the road is always a possibility. Be alert for cattle guards—short sections of parallel pipes running perpendicular to the road—which are designed to keep live-

➡ Average Texas Temperatures

★	Austin	Brownsville	Corpus Christi	Dallas - Fort Worth	El Paso	Galveston	Houston	San Antonio
Jan	60-41	71-52	67-47	56-36	56-32	60-48	62-46	62-42
Feb	63-44	73-59	70-56	60-39	62-37	63-51	66-50	66-45
Mar	71-49	77-59	74-56	67-45	68-41	67-56	71-54	71-45
Apr	78-57	82-66	80-63	75-55	77-50	74-64	78-61	79-58
May	85-65	87-71	85-69	83-63	86-58	81-71	85-67	85-65
Jun	92-74	91-75	91-74	91-72	94-67	87-77	90-74	92-72
Jul	95-74	93-75	94-75	95-75	94-69	89-79	92-75	94-74
Aug	96-74	93-75	94-75	95-75	92-68	89-79	93-75	92-73
Sep	90-69	90-73	90-71	88-67	88-62	85-79	89-71	89-69
Oct	82-60	85-67	85-65	79-57	79-52	79-68	82-63	82-60
Nov	70-48	77-58	74-54	66-44	66-38	69-57	71-53	70-49
Dec	63-43	72-54	69-50	58-38	58-33	63-51	64-47	65-42

Temperatures: max-min

stock from crossing into a new area. Texas also has a healthy deer population, especially in the hill country.

Note that many rural roads in Texas have broad paved shoulders on each side. When being overtaken by faster traffic, locals commonly maintain their speed, but pull over to these shoulders—a nice gesture. Don't be shy about passing slower vehicles like this, and return the favor when you are being overtaken.

You will see two signs often in Texas: DRIVE FRIENDLY and DON'T MESS WITH TEXAS; the first is self-evident, and the second is a coy roadside attempt to keep our fair state looking its best. Both are good advice.

*Texans are proud
of their heritage
and most small
towns have
monuments in the
square.*

A Proud History

The colorful history of Texas makes it what it is today. This chapter will give you a short summary of the story. The size of the state and the different backgrounds of the various regions give each area a particular history of its own. Each individual riding chapter includes a short explanation of the local character, to show what makes that region unique.

Of course, long before Europeans arrived, roaming tribes of Indians inhabited the region. They left little impact on history because they were either killed or run out of the region by new settlers.

After the Spanish conquistadores discovered the vast riches of Mexico and Peru, they turned their interest north, actively seeking more treasure in the "new world." The first extensive exploration of this area was led by Francisco Vasquez de Coronado in 1540. He and his men roamed much of Texas, going as far north as present-day Kansas. To encourage the Spanish to move on, the Indians always told stories of great cities of gold in far-off, remote locations. After two years of being led on wild goose chases, Coronado and his men returned to Mexico City.

In 1542 another Spanish expedition exploring east Texas discovered a black, slimy substance that smelled bad, but would burn. Although they did not realize it, this crude oil would become the "gold" of Texas. In the middle of the 18th century, Spain tried to settle and cultivate these lands while converting the Indians to Christianity. They established a series of missions and forts *(presidios)* in Texas. The Indians resented the intrusion and threat to their way of life. A series of successful attacks stopped further expansion and caused the Spanish to retrench. The most famous of these old missions, Mision San Antonio de Valero, was established in present-day San Antonio and became a real factor in the future of Texas. Today, this mission is better known as the Alamo.

The Mexican people won their independence from Spain in a bloody revolution in 1821, and the area known as Texas became the northernmost state of the new country. Lacking resources other than raw land, the Mexican government made large land grants, called *empresarios,* to U.S. and European citizens in order to encourage settlement of the area. Promises of almost free land and unlimited potential for development brought scores of U.S. citizens south into Texas. Many of the first settlers moved to Texas to

The Texas state flag is most often flown on a separate flagpole and at a height equal to the U.S. flag, indicating the widespread belief that the nation of Texas is equal in importance to the United States.

escape hanging or lesser criminal penalties. Others left wives and children behind and "escaped" the bonds of civilization. Most, however, were honest, hard working people looking to better their lot in life. They formed the bedrock of the new society.

While obtaining land in Mexican Texas was cheap, it did have drawbacks. To obtain land, you had to become Catholic, renounce your U.S. citizenship, and pledge your loyalty to Mexico. All official documents had to be in Spanish. The new citizens, called Texicans, soon began talking of revolt and forming their own country. In 1833, the Mexican government decreed that no more U.S. citizens would be accepted into Texas.

In 1835 the Texicans declared their independence from Mexico and General Antonio Lopez de Santa Anna amassed an army and marched north to put down the upstart rebellion. The first battle took place at a mission near San Antonio called the Alamo. An army of more than 5,000 Mexicans surrounded 189 Texicans who fought bravely and held off attempts to overrun the Alamo. After twelve days and 2,000 Mexican casualties, the mission fell and all its defenders were killed. Their defeat proved to be a rallying point for the rest of the Texicans and the battle cry became, "Remember the Alamo!"

Another event that fueled the Texicans fight-to-the-death attitude occurred in the town of Goliad on March 27,1836. A few days earlier, a group of approximately 400 Texicans surrendered to the Mexican army after a heated battle. On this Palm Sunday morning, Santa Anna ordered approximately 350 prisoners executed, more lives than were lost at the Alamo. This massacre of unarmed men gave life to another battle cry, "Remember Goliad!"

➡ Texas Rangers

As law enforcement officers, Texas Rangers are known the world over, a reputation they have earned throughout their storied history, which is rooted in their early attempts to enforce the law along the border. The Mexicans of the 1800s called the rangers *los diablos tejanos,* the Texan devils! The rangers were known to shoot first and ask questions later. Let's just say that protecting the civil rights of a Mexican caught with a few "stray" cattle did not rate high on their list of priorities.

Using similar tactics, the rangers are credited with running the wild Indian tribes from the state, as well as protecting settlers from outlaws. Once, when a town had been overrun by bad guys, the governor was asked to send help to stop the riot. When a single ranger arrived, the city fathers asked, "Only one ranger?" To which the ranger replied, "There is only one riot isn't there?"

It is probably safe to say that most of the early rangers would not be welcome in your living room today. During the Mexican-American war, General Taylor was incensed by the behavior of the rangers. They would kill at any chance and had no regard for the lives of their victims. However, Taylor wanted them at the front in all attacks because they proved themselves up to any task. The early rangers served six-month enlistments and were often not supplied by the government with necessary food and supplies. They solved this problem by "obtaining" any requirements on the spot and promising that the government would reimburse the owner later.

Today, the Texas Rangers are a small, elite force limited to no more than 99 in number. While their primary purpose is guarding the state governor, they also handle white-collar crime investigations and are called out for other special tasks as needed or requested. Texans will speak with great pride of the job Captain Barry Caver did in handling a standoff with Richard McLaren and his followers in 1997. All hostages were released and the group finally surrendered without any loss of life. Compare that to a similar situation handled by the federal government: the debacle in Waco, Texas.   ★

The Mexican army, which had experienced heavy losses, had to maintain long and difficult supply lines. When the two opposing armies met in San Jacinto (near Houston) on April 21, 1836 the Texicans had their victory and freedom. Santa Anna was captured and held for several days. In spite of public sentiment, Sam Houston, leader of the Texican forces, refused to have him killed. It is rumored that Santa Anna had been slow to enter the battle because he'd been enjoying the intimate company of a mulatto woman. The unofficial anthem of the Lone Star State, *The Yellow Rose of Texas,* was written in her honor.

A stop at the location of the famous Spindletop oil discovery is a "must."

The republic of Texas lasted only a short ten years before joining the United States. Sam Houston was elected as its first president in September 1836. He and the new republic faced the same difficulties as the Mexicans: lots of land, few people, and almost no money. Cheap land grants encouraged immigration, especially from areas of Europe that had problems of their own. Even today, regions of Texas developed by settlers from Germany and elsewhere have retained unique flavors and heritages.

Meanwhile, Texas continued to battle Indian uprisings as well as constant border disputes with Mexico. The republic needed help, and in 1846 Texas was granted statehood, earning the official assistance of the U.S. government and its troops. The Mexican-American War (1846–48) was a huge disaster for Mexico and U.S. troops went as far as capturing Mexico City. When the dust had settled, Mexico had given up its claim to the lands of present-day Texas, California, Utah, Colorado and most of Arizona and New Mexico—almost one-half of its territory. As a result, the famous General Santa Anna was exiled for life from his home country.

As word of the seemingly unlimited land and opportunities in the new state spread, settlers poured in from both the eastern U.S. and Europe. Today Texas has the largest Czech population in the world outside of Czechoslovakia. Eastern Texas became a major cotton-producing state as plantation owners from the American South moved from depleted lands of their eastern plantations to the "new" soil of Texas. During the Civil War, Texas sided with the Confederacy and was a major supplier of food and cotton for export. Spurred by the conflict, large-scale cattle production—and the legend of the Texan cowboy—was born.

When most people think of Texas history, they picture cowboys, cattle, lawlessness, and gunfights. Its popularity with Hollywood not withstanding, the wild era of ranchers and outlaws really lasted only about 40 years or so (1860–1900) and was soon squelched by civilizing forces. Continued immigration from more settled states and countries brought about an agricultural boom and the Texas "wheeler-dealer" soon made his appearance to claim a piece of the growing pie. But the expansion of the railroads into cow country ended the need for long drives and barbed wire made it possible to fence off great areas of land at minimal cost.

Civilization may have tamed Texas, but its wild roots run deep. Texans have proudly absorbed this legacy into their daily outlook and you will see it expressed in many ways, from their willingness to take risks, both in life and business, to their generally "loose" attitude toward following The Rules.

We cannot speak of Texas without mentioning oil and its influence. Oil wells were drilled in east Texas as early as 1866. As several small fields were discovered, the business expanded slowly into other parts of the state. Not many uses for oil and oil products existed at the time. In 1901 a well that was drilled near Beaumont, in an area known as Spindletop, would affect the oil industry for nearly 70 years. This well, a "gusher," came in as no other had ever before. When it was finally under control, it could produce more than 80,000 barrels of oil per day—an unprecedented amount. Soon drillers, wildcatters, wheeler-dealers, and lots of other people looking to make money headed to Texas. The era of the oil-field boomtowns must have been quite a sight to see. Tales of whores, gambling dens, saloons, shootings, knifings, and other unsavory activities abound.

By the 1960's, while oil was still king, the Texas economy was starting to diversify as people flocked to Texas, attracted by the warm climate, inexpensive housing, friendly reputation, and opportunities to get a piece of the pie. As it is known in Texas, this "Yankee Invasion" did little to change attitudes in the state. Most new arrivals promptly got a pair of cowboy boots and a pickup truck and were soon absorbed into the culture. While still leader of the House, Lyndon Johnson was a master in the art of "pork barrel" politics. He managed to get several military bases located in Texas and was instrumental in NASA's decision to locate its headquarters near Houston. This obviously attracted many other high-tech companies with huge government contracts to move to the state. True to their nature, Texans soon became experts in land and real estate speculation.

In 1973, the Organization of Petroleum Exporting Countries imposed an oil embargo on the United States and its allies for their pro-Israeli policies. While this was a blow to the western economies, it created a boom for Texas and other oil producing states. The demand for crude oil in the U.S. exceeded domestic production capacity and a true shortage soon developed. Crude oil prices quickly doubled, tripled, and climbed even higher.

A gold rush mentality took over Texas and the oil industry. Banks loaned money to construct drilling rigs, pipelines, barges, and refineries, all based on the false assumption that the price of crude oil and oil products would continue to rise. Mexico, also a major oil producer, experienced the same boom, and Texas received an influx of pesos from Mexican nationals as they flocked to cities like Houston to spend their newly found wealth and invest in Texas real estate. Massive upscale shopping malls and world-class hotels were constructed to handle the new tourist base. Restaurants and other service industries flourished.

Gradually, consumers reacted to the higher energy prices by becoming more energy efficient. Small, fuel-efficient Japanese automobiles became so popular that they nearly drove American manufacturers out of business before they could retool and meet the competition. As alternative sources of energy gained ground, the new oil fields that had been developed at the inflated prices lost their value. OPEC countries started to suffer from a cash flow crisis because of the embargo. They quietly began selling larger and larger volumes, and the embargo was effectively over. As a result, an oil glut replaced the shortages in the early 1980s. The price of crude oil dropped like a brick.

The Texas economy reeled. Tourists from Mexico no longer came and many new high-rise office towers and other projects were stopped in mid-construction. The banking industry suffered major blows as loans based on an estimated crude oil value of over $40 a barrel were called in and sold at $10 a barrel. Hundreds of oil and oil service companies went bankrupt. The good times were over.

Texans reacted to this problem true to the form of their forefathers. They picked themselves up, dusted off their pants, and went in search of the next opportunity. By the early 1990s Texans had diversified their economy away from the oil industry, although it still plays an important role. Their high-tech industry rivals California's famous Silicon Valley. With the passing of NAFTA, business with Mexico increased and Texas led all states in population growth during the '90s.

One can only wonder what Texas will do next.

➡ Texas Political Sayings

At the end of president George W. Bush's term in 2004, Texas natives or adopted sons have held the White House for twenty-two of the last fifty-one years: Dwight Eisenhower (8 years), Lyndon Johnson (6 years), George H. Bush (4 years) and George W. Bush (4 years).

Texas politics are as rough and tumble as you will find anywhere in the country. As Senator Lloyd Benson explained when he made what some thought were totally uncalled-for remarks about his vice-presidential debate opponent Dan Quayle, "In Texas, politics is considered a contact sport."

Since the state is evenly split between the major parties, it's hard to predict who will be dominant after each election. Texas is the birthplace of the Independent party founder Ross Perot. Here are a few of the more memorable remarks you could have heard over the years:

"When I was young and stupid, I was young and stupid."
-George W. Bush

"If you grab them by their balls, their hearts and minds will follow."
-Lyndon Johnson

"Texas could get along without the United States, but the United States cannot, except with great hazard, exist without Texas."
-Sam Houston

"If ignorance ever goes to forty dollars a barrel, I want drillin' rights on that man's head."
-Jim Hightower, Texas Agriculture Commissioner, discussing President George H. Bush

"What we need now is a good hurricane."
-Governor Bill Clements, after an oil spill had polluted some Texas beaches

And finally, an all-time favorite, attributed to an unknown candidate as the shortest campaign speech in Texas history: "Fellow citizens, follow me into yonder saloon."   ✪

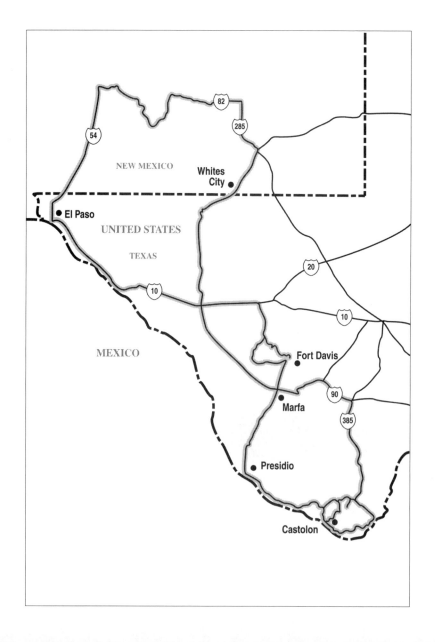

El Paso The Wild West

Beginning and ending in El Paso, this six or seven day route of approximately 1,100 miles will take you through some of the most remote areas in the lower 48 states. The vastness of west Texas can be overwhelming and occasional stops alongside the road gives a person time to reflect on one's small place in the world. You'll be within range of some bona fide natural wonders, and visits to towns of less than one-thousand inhabitants will give you some insight into the sort of people who have chosen this lonely, wide open space as their home.

In the 1500s, this area was "discovered" by the Spanish in their ongoing search for gold. Its desert environment and sheer remoteness made it one of the last parts of Texas to become civilized. Outlaws, bandits, gunslingers, and other ne'er-do-wells controlled the area until 1916 when the U.S. Army under the command of **General "Black Jack" Pershing** took control at Fort Bliss. Their mission was to protect the border with Mexico, but their final legacy was in bringing order to the area.

El Paso sits in a valley with the Franklin mountains invitingly close by. (photo by J. Griffis/TxDOT)

Today, west Texas still contains immense open spaces with some of the sparsest population densities in the United States, as well as the world's largest bi-national metropolis, **El Paso-Juárez,** with a population approaching three million people. The two cities in the metropolis exist as one, with constant traffic between the two during all hours of the day. U.S. citizens cross the border to obtain less expensive health care and goods, as well as to enjoy the freer lifestyles of Mexico; Mexican citizens come to El Paso to obtain goods and services not available on the Mexican side.

With the implementation of the North American Free Trade Agreement, many factories, called *maquiladoras,* have been built with U.S. capital and management to take advantage of cheaper labor rates of Mexico. Unlike other cities in Texas, El Paso does not have a major tourist draw, but people come to El Paso to enjoy easy access to Mexico and the remote desert. The

Today's cowboy boots, while still maintaining their original, functional design, are most often only a fashion statement. (photo by J. Griffis Smith/TxDOT)

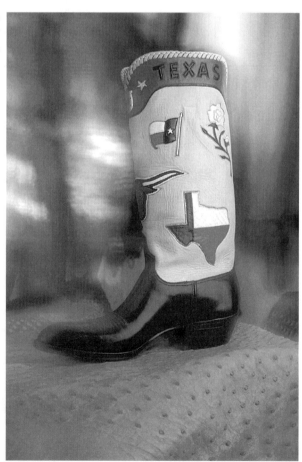

➡ Cowboy Boots

The cowboy boot originated in Spain, migrated to Mexico and found its home in Texas. They were originally designed to be a functional piece of rugged footwear: the pointed toe makes it easy to put your foot in a stirrup, the heel gives you some stability while riding, and the high tops are meant to protect the wearer from thorns and other hazards of the range. Today, of course, the cowboy boot has become a fashion statement. Until the 1960s, almost all cowboy boots were handmade. Today, Texas is the world's leader in cowboy boot production. One company alone has annual sales of more than three million pairs. In Paris, Texas, there is even a tombstone with a statue of Jesus wearing cowboy boots.

The cost of a pair of boots is first determined by whether they are factory or hand made. Custom fitting and your choice of materials and designs will all contribute to the cost. A good, "off the shelf" pair will probably be $200–300; a serviceable hand-made pair will be a little more expensive, but not much. Of course, top-of-the-line cowboy boots made with detailed inlays and exotic skins, such as ostrich, eel, or anaconda, can run $5,000 or more. Two of the more popular designs include the Texas Lone Star and derricks gushing crude oil. Because of the high demand, custom boot orders from the best craftsmen can take more than a year to fill. ★

Franklin Mountains, at the end of the Rockies chain, form the northern boundary of the city and they offer wonderful opportunities for the residents to enjoy the rugged outdoors.

El Paso is the **cowboy boot capitol of the world.** If you hanker for a set of boots at a good price, try **Cowtown Boots** at 11451 Gateway West. With more than 40,000 square feet of western wear, they have something for everyone. Craftsmen in the "bootmaking" district of El Paso, located along S. Cotton Street, offer custom-made creations that can top $10,000 a pair.

If possible, you should take a ride on the **Trans Mountain Loop** (Loop 375) that goes across the Franklin Mountains and through **Franklin Mountains State Park.** Take I-10 west to Exit 6 (Canutilo) and follow it to its conclusion at the intersection with Hwy. 54. Take a right here and you will re-enter El Paso on the eastern side. The total ride is about 32 miles, downtown to downtown, and the 12-mile loop road itself is a delight. The climb to almost 7,000 feet has pull-offs overlooking the twin cities.

Two interesting sites are situated almost side by side on the eastern end of the Trans Mountain Loop. The first is the **Border Patrol Museum** (4315 Trans Mountain Road), which outlines the history of this organization and

Texas steakhouses try and live up to the reputation that "everything" is bigger in Texas. (photo by Bob Parvin/TxDOT)

houses exhibits of items confiscated from people trying to enter the United States illegally. Second is the **Wilderness Park Museum** at 4332 Trans Mountain Road. It exhibits the flora of the desert, that you will soon visit along a self-guided outdoor trail. It also has an indoor section that details the lives of the early Indian inhabitants.

Another way to visit the Franklin Mountains is to take the **Wyler Aerial Tramway,** which has been completely renovated since its original construction in the 1960s. Guides point out the various sights while you enjoy the spectacular views. From the visitors' center, you can see New Mexico and the Mexican state of Chihuahua. To get to the tram, take Alabama to McKinley Avenue and turn toward the mountain. McKinley Avenue ends at the base of the tram. Take Hwy. 54 to the Fred Wilson exit to hook up with Alabama.

➡ Just How Dry is West Texas?

The amount of rainfall received in Texas varies greatly. In the east, more than fifty inches a year is common. This diminishes steadily as you move west, and west Texas receives only a few inches per year. Starting at about the Dallas-Fort Worth area, there would not be enough rainfall to support agriculture or cattle if it were not for huge, underground lakes, called aquifers, whose water levels are carefully monitored and guarded. Historically, water rights are precious and they have been the subject of lawsuits or shootings. When you are out and about, be sure to stay adequately hydrated.   ★

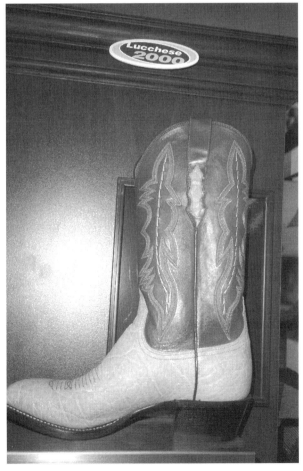

This boot will never find its way to a real cowboy's foot.

➡ Cowboys

While the cowboy played a brief but important role in Texas, Hollywood has inflated their true significance completely out of proportion with history. Even at their peak, cowboys represented only a minuscule portion of the population.

After the Civil War, Texas had both vast, free-roaming herds of cattle and a growing market for them in the east. The rough and rugged men who rounded up these herds to drive them to the nearest railroad claimed their stock by branding them. A cowboy's life was difficult, and the work hard and dirty. At the end of a drive, they would draw their pay and let their hair down in wild towns where just about anything could happen, and often did, giving rise to yet another historical icon, that of the Texas lawman.

With the advent of barbed wire and the extension of the railroads, long cattle drives became obsolete and the cowboy all but disappeared from the landscape—but not the silver screen. Today, you will see lots of Texans wearing cowboy boots and hats, but few cowboys. ✪

Another short ride that can provide you with a real sense of history is the **Mission Trail.** Take I-10 east from downtown to the Zaragoza exit. Turn right on Zaragoza to Old Pueblo Road, which will place you on the clearly marked trail in Ysleta. **Ysleta del Sur Pueblo** offers quite a contrast to the visitor, with the oldest mission in Texas sitting right next to a huge casino complex. The **Tigua Cultural Center,** Home of the Tigua Indian tribe, at 305 Yaya Lane, gives wonderful insight into the lives of these people and how they have managed to retain their culture over the years. Two miles further east on the trail (Hwy. 20), you will come to the **Socorro Mission,** the oldest continually active parish in the United States (est. 1681). Another five miles east, the small town of San Elizario contains the **San Elzario Presido.** A visit to the church established here in 1877 and a stroll about the town square will remind you of many similar small towns in Mexico.

El Paso offers lodgings in every price range with most of the national chains represented in the airport area. There are also many "mom and pop" motels near the airport that provide cheap, basic lodging. If you would like a place that is somewhat out of the ordinary, try the **Cliff Inn** ($65; 915-533-6700, 800-333-2543) at 1600 Cliff Dr. Located in the Franklin Mountains, but still near downtown, the ambiance of the place helps you overlook the somewhat threadbare rooms. Camping is available at the **El Paso Roadrunner Travel Trailer Park** at 1212 Yarbrough Dr. (take the Yarbrough exit off I-10) for $18 per night. It has all the amenities, including showers, laundry, and a grocery store.

Your dining options are almost limitless in and around El Paso. Not only is it the self-proclaimed **Mexican Food Capitol of the U.S.**, it is also renowned for its steak houses. One of my favorite places for carving up a cow can be found on the western outskirts of town. The **State Line,** so named because the border between New Mexico and Texas runs through the middle of the place, is located off I-10 west of downtown at 1222 Sunland Park Drive. If you have a hearty appetite, consider one of their all-you-can-eat platters—just make sure you will be able to remount your bike when you're done.

Day 1   El Paso to Fort Davis

Distance *210 miles*

Features *Although the first 150 miles of interstate riding are not the high-point of this trip, you'll begin to get a real feel for the endless desert highlands before turning south into the Davis Mountains. From there, you will enjoy wonderful up-and-down twisties. As you approach 7,000 feet you will leave the desert behind for rugged forests. Note that you will enter the Central Time Zone shortly before passing Van Horn at Exit 140.*

The tour through the McDonald Observatory will have your mind reeling at vastness of the universe.

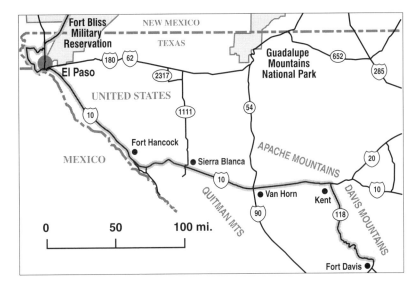

From El Paso, get on I-10 east. If you arrive in El Paso late in the day and just want to put a few miles behind you, I recommend stopping fifty miles into this stretch, in the town of Fort Hancock (Exit 72). The **Fort Hancock Motel** ($30; 915-769-3981), just off the interstate on the right, is a good clean "mom and pop" place. Ask for a room in the rear. Standing outside your room in the evening, the view of the mountains in the distance and the yelping of coyotes will let you know that you have arrived in west Texas!

Across the street from the Fort Hancock is the non-descript **Angie's Café.** While this place is a hole-in-the-wall, the food is wonderful and it has been written up in *National Geographic Explorer, Texas Monthly* and other well-regarded travel publications. If you plan to eat only one chicken-fried steak on your trip, this is the place!

Continue on I-10 to Exit 176 at Kent. Turn south on Hwy.118. After 20 miles or so, you enter the Davis Mountains and pass the **University of Texas McDonald Observatory** on your left, at an altitude of nearly 7,000 feet, before descending into the town of Fort Davis for the night. At just over 5,000 feet, Fort Davis is the highest city in Texas. I recommend you stop at the observatory on your way by to see which tours and activities might best fit your schedule tomorrow.

As you enter Fort Davis, you will soon see the **Hotel Limpia** ($90; 915-426-3118, 800-662-5517) on your left at the town square. This delightfully restored hotel was originally built in 1884 near the site of the fort itself, but was moved to its "new" location in 1912, where it provided lodging for rich folks from the hot flatlands seeking cool air in the summertime. Although it has been finished throughout in period décor from the early 1900s, the rooms have all the modern conveniences. The adjoining restaurant offers great dining at a level you might not expect to find in such a small town.

As an alternative, check out the **Old Texas Inn** ($45; 915-426-3118, 800-328-4748), located on the main drag as you enter town above the **Fort Davis Drug Store,** which now serves as a souvenir stand and a local café that serves up some good ol' west Texas cooking. There are several other more standard motels in this town, but a stay in either these will give you a taste of what it was like in this area at the turn of the century.

If you are camping, follow Hwy. 118 through Fort Davis. The **Davis Mountains State Park,** only six miles down this road, offers a wonderful atmosphere on the **Limpia River.** All sites have water, a barbeque grill, and tables. Hot showers and restrooms are available. The nearby **Indian Lodge Motel** has adequate dining facilities.

The town of **Fort Davis** (pop. 1,300) was founded in 1854 on the **Overland Trail** between San Antonio and El Paso. It must have been a pleasant stop for the many settlers, gold seekers, and others heading west to find better times, as they left the crushing heat of the desert and ascended to these cooler altitudes. Even today, its economy supports the many tourists seeking an opportunity to get out of their air-conditioned environments and enjoy the outdoors during the summer months. A short stroll off the main street will

It sure looks like some excellent riding is ahead in the Davis Mountains! (photo by Jack Binion)

By stopping by and visiting the Fort Davis National Historical Site, you gain real insights into life on the frontier. (photo by Richard Reynolds/TxDOT)

allow you to see how the residents lived in the old days, with traditional adobe houses still in use today.

Day 2   Fort Davis to Presidio

Distance *155 miles*

Features *This 72-mile loop through the Davis Mountains will give you ample chance to twist your wrist and scrape your pegs, though a more leisurely pace will allow for roadside stops to soak in the beautiful mountain scenery. I recommend you get off your bike to visit Fort Davis (a National Historical Landmark) and the University of Texas McDonald Observatory (see details below). A 60-mile run through remote high desert will put you in the small town of Presidio at the Mexican border.*

This rider appears to be contemplating a U-turn to ride the Davis Mountain loop again— tempting!

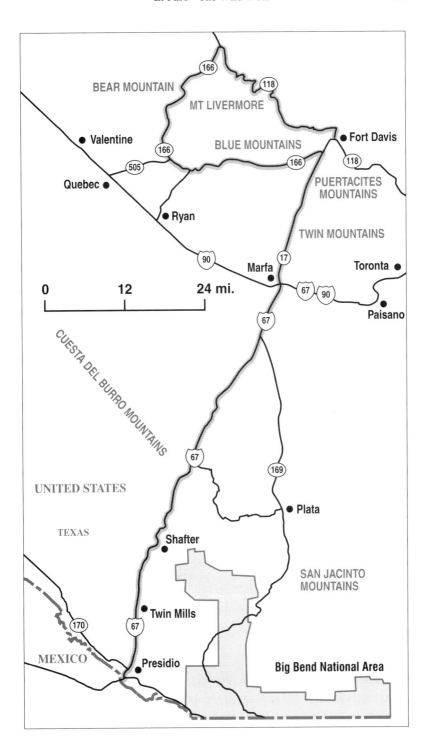

Leave town the way you came in, and at the outskirts, on your left, the **restored Fort Davis** awaits your visit. As more people began using the **Overland Trail** from San Antonio to El Paso, raids from the Apache and Comanche Indians became a problem. In 1854 the U.S. Army established a fort near the Limpia River to escort wagon trains through the area, pursue Indian raiders, and guard the mail. Named in honor of **Jefferson Davis,** the Secretary of War at the time, the facility was built of cottonwood, scrub oak, and pine; today only the foundations of the original fort remain. It was abandoned, occupied by Confederates during the Civil War, and abandoned again before being reconstructed in adobe and stone in 1867. The famous **"buffalo soldiers,"** all-black units with white officers, occupied the fort during the 1870s and '80s. It was closed in 1891.

In 1961 Fort Davis was designated as a **National Historic Site** and has been faithfully restored as one of the best surviving examples of a southwestern frontier military post. A nice museum is located inside, and a short film tracing the history of the fort is shown throughout the day. You are welcome to roam at will.

After your visit, continue to retrace yesterday's route for about 15 miles. The **University of Texas McDonald Observatory** complex will be on your right. It is hard to miss, as you can spot the enormous buildings containing the telescopes for miles before arriving. At an altitude of approximately 6,800 feet, the observatory is located in one of the "darkest" parts of the United States (i.e. little interference from man-made artificial light sources). The 13.5-million dollar **Hobby Eberly Telescope,** dedicated in October of 1997, contains 91 hexagonal mirrors over a 36-foot wide surface and is the world's largest mirror telescope. Time on the telescopes is booked months and years in advance by researchers from all over the world. Since the facility cannot be used during daylight hours for scientific study, the time is set aside to give guided tours to the general public.

To learn the schedule of the many interesting events offered at the observatory, call 915-426-3640. Most presentations are on a first-come, first-served basis and rarely are full, but evening **"star parties"** often require reservations well in advance. Note that if you want to attend one of the latter, be extremely careful riding to and from the site after dark, as wildlife is copious and the road leading up to the site, known as **Skyline Drive,** is the highest paved road in Texas. With all the clear air, it seems you can see forever.

From this point, another 15 miles north on Hwy. 118 will bring you to the intersection of Hwy. 166, a scenic loop which will return you to the town of Fort Davis after 45 miles or so. Just outside Fort Davis you will come to a T-intersection with Hwy. 17; turn right toward Marfa, only 20 miles down the

This biker can only hope he doesn't encounter the cowboy who fits these spurs. (photo by Jack Binion)

road. At this point, the **Davis Mountains** will be in your rear view mirror as you cross pastureland and farms. The huge greenhouses along this drive are **hydroponic tomato farms** which specialize in a hybrid variety named after Fort Davis.

Follow Hwy. 17 signs through Marfa until you intersect with Hwy. 67. Take Hwy. 67 south toward Presidio. This is a quick 59-mile ride through the desert with mountains jutting up on every side and Mexico straight ahead. Approximately 35 miles south of Marfa, a dirt road off to the right leads to the much-acclaimed **Cibolo Creek Ranch,** a truly wonderful 25,000-acre dude ranch. At more than $300 per night (includes meals), it should be good. Developed by **Milton Faver** in the mid-19th century, the ranch contains a series of forts surrounding the main ranch house for protec-

Be sure to take some time out from your ride through west Texas to enjoy the scenery.

tion from the Indians and bandits. It is now a popular retreat for celebrities and the rich.

Past the ranch turnoff the road becomes more interesting with nice curves and gently rolling hills. In Presidio, the **Three Palms Hotel** ($40; 915-229-3611), located on old Hwy. 67 north, is more than adequate. Next door to the motel is **Rosie's,** a cafe which is very popular with locals and serves up some good Tex-Mex food. Primitive camping is available only a short distance to the east on Hwy. 170 in the **Big Bend Ranch State Park** near the Fort Leaton State Historic Site. The campsite has pit toilets only, but water and showers are available.

Presidio (pop. 4,000) is known as the hottest town in Texas. Its twin on the Mexico side is Ojinaga and the two towns co-exist as if one. This is the only official border crossing point between El Paso and Del Rio, a 450-mile stretch. The area contains fertile floodplains and is famous for its farming. It is the self-proclaimed **Onion Capitol of the World.** It is important as the western entryway to **El Camino del Rio** (River Road), which has been touted as one of the ten best motorcycle roads in the United States.

✪ *Side Trip*

Should you wish to visit Mexico, the town of **Ojinaga** (pop. 40,000) is just across the river from Presidio and no paperwork is required if you plan to stay less than 72 hours. The easiest way to visit Ojinaga is to take the **Ruta Presidio-OJ. Shuttle** ($2) from MB's supermarket on the main road in Presidio. As an alternative, a cab will cost about five dollars.

Ojinaga is not a tourist town, but has a thriving international trade. Try eating "real" Mexican food at **Chuco's** (Av Trasviña y Retes and Calle 13) or better yet, enjoy **Mini-Chucao's** outside and watch the world go by. If you decide to visit Ojinaga, stop by **Panderia La Francesa** on Calle Zaragoza near the town plaza and stock up on sweets for your late night snack or morning meal.

Day 3   Presidio to Big Bend National Park

Distance *120 miles*

Features *Don't let the distance fool you. You will be stopping often and spending much time on the side of the road enjoying the magnificent landscape. The 50-mile stretch from Presidio to Lajitas curves constantly as it follows the path of the Rio Grande River. The steepest hill in Texas climbs a 16-percent grade to a height of 5,000 feet. After reaching Study Butte you will enter the Big Bend National Park with its astonishing terrain and roads. The day ends in the Chisos Basin.*

From looking at this sign, it would appear these riders have been having a good time. (courtesy of Pancho Villa Moto-Tours)

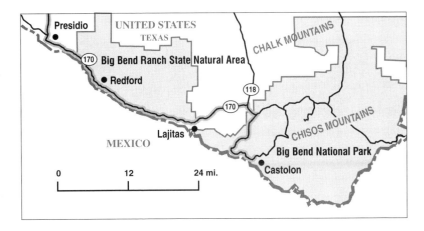

Depart the motel, return to Hwy. 170 and continue for 67 miles on Hwy. 170 eastward to Study Butte. This road from Presido to Study Butte is often mentioned by various publications as **one of the ten most scenic roads** in the United States, and most motorcyclists would agree with the designation. After 46 miles of delightful riding, you'll see an abandoned movie set on your right where they filmed *The Streets of Laredo* and *Dead Man's Walk.* This makes for a nice little stop as you can stroll the set and pretend to have stepped backward in time.

Just after the set you will encounter "the hill." At a 16-percent grade, this hill is the steepest in Texas and the road peaks at an altitude of more than 5,000 feet. There is a nice pull-off at the summit and only the hard-core, no-photos-please rider will be able to resist the urge to burn a good deal of film there. Walk over the summit and get the view ahead before remounting your bike for the five-mile run to Lajitas.

The small outpost of **Lajitas** was established because it had an easy crossing over the **Rio Grande River,** and over the years it served this purpose well for Indians, traders, and *banditos* alike. In the early 1900s **General "Black Jack" Pershing** established a U.S. Cavalry post here to deal with **Pancho Villa** and his band.

Today, the original town is overshadowed by Lajitas on the Rio Grande, a resort that consists of a period-style square containing several stores, restaurants, a hotel, apartments, and condos. An eighteen-hole golf course is connected to the resort. The "real" Lajitas, however, still exists and continues to do well. Turn right just before the resort complex and follow a dirt road approximately one block to the old **Lajitas Trading Post,** which offers a varied selection of hardware and groceries. Many Mexicans cross the river to do their shopping here.

This resort area in Lajitas makes for a nice stop with several good restaurants, a recreated "old west" hotel and plenty of shopping opportunities. (photo by Richard Reynolds/TxDOT).

Several years back, in a hotly contested mayoral race, the citizens of Lajitas chose a goat named **Henry Clay** as the winner. Henry's main claim to fame, other than being mayor, was his ability to consume vast quantities of beer. Henry died, some say of liver failure, and was succeeded by his son, **Henry, Jr.** Unfortunately, Henry Jr. eventually met the same fate. The grandson, **Henry Clay III** carries on the family tradition today, although a former political opponent, frustrated after losing election after election to a goat, decided to vent his spleen by castrating Henry III in hopes that it would put an end to this political dynasty.

From Lajitias it is only 17 miles to the intersection with Farm Road 118 at Study Butte where a right turn toward the **Big Bend National Park** will soon bring you to its western entrance. About 4 miles before Study Butte you pass an area known as **Terlingua.** This is not a clearly defined location, but rather a scattering of abandoned buildings and run-down adobe shacks, some of which are still occupied even without the benefit of running water or electricity. The area's main claims to fame are its **annual chili cook-offs,** which occur on two weekends each year and attract crowds estimated at more than 10,000. The rest of the year, it is a popular destination for mountain bikers. The post office in Study Butte has a schedule of current and upcoming local activities.

After passing the entrance booth into the park, take an immediate right turn onto Old Maverick Road. This is 13 miles of well-maintained dirt that is easily traveled by any bike with competent rider. Take a minute to dismount six or seven miles down this road. The silence will overwhelm most people. Think of the hardships that must have been incurred trying to cross this empty desert land on a horse or wagon.

When you intersect with pavement again, turn right for a mile or so to the dead-end at **Santa Elena Canyon.** A short hike allows you to climb up and into the canyon, which was cut by the **Rio Grande River.** Its sheer cliffs, which reach more than 1,500 feet above the Rio Grande, and narrow passages will amaze you. Plan on spending some time here to explore and enjoy. Should you not wish to ride this short dirt portion, continue on pavement for 13 miles to Santa Elena Junction and make a right turn. It is then 30 paved miles to the Santa Elena Canyon.

After enjoying the wonderful sights and sounds of Santa Elena, take the paved road out and return 30 miles to the main road, turn right here and continue about 10 miles to the right turn off to the **Chisos Basin.** The road out of Santa Elena to the main road is an absolute pleasure, with sprinklings of buttes and broad valleys. There are several well-marked pull-offs along this road provided by the park service with informative signs. One of the best is the **Mule Ears viewpoint.**

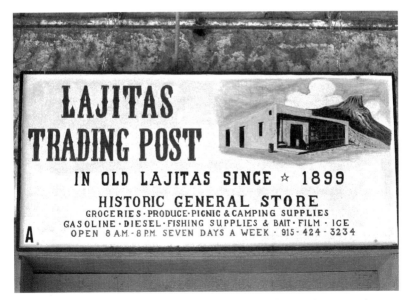

This is not a tourist trap, but a genuine general store in Lajitas. (courtesy of Pancho Villa Moto-Tours)

A stop at the Lajitas Trading Post is a must. Be sure and become acquainted with the town's mayor, Henry Clay III, a goat.

The short walk into the massive Santa Elena Canyon is an awe-inspiring experience. (photo by Jack Binion)

If the entranceway booth was closed as you entered the park, proceed straight ahead. At the Chisos Basin, turn another 3 miles to the **Panther Junction Visitors' Center** to get your admission tickets, before continuing back to the **Chisos Lodge** for your overnight accommodations. At the park headquarters at Panther Junction you can obtain brochures, maps, and other information that will make your visit more enjoyable.

If you already have paid the entrance fee, the same information is available at the **Basin Information Center and Museum.** The short, 6-mile ride into the basin is a beautiful motorcycle road that climbs up over the mountain. It is quite tight at some places and even has a couple of switchbacks. The **Chisos Mountains Lodge** ($80; 915-477-2291) is the only available place to overnight in the park (excluding campsites) and offers a dramatic setting. It has 72 motel-type rooms and a few stone cottages located only a short walk away. Deer, wild pigs, and other wildlife can be seen in the early evenings and mornings as you walk to the basic, but adequate, dining room.

Roads in the Big Bend Park offer frequent pull-offs containing interesting exhibits. (photo by Jack Binion).

At times, most notably during Spring Break, the place can be filled; it is best to call ahead and reserve a room.

Camping is available in Big Bend on a first-come basis at Rio Grande Village, Chisos Basin, and Costolon, at a cost of $7 per night. All "formal" campsites have showers and water. Chisos Basin offers high-country camping with a lodge and café located just up the hill. It also has a well-stocked store to meet most of your needs. Rio Grande, as the name implies is located on the banks of the Rio Grande River, nestled among trees. Backcountry campsites are free, but do require a permit. Before spending the night at a remote campsite, make sure you get current information at the ranger station.

Big Bend National Park is often called **The Last Frontier of Texas** (info 915-477-2251; res. 915-477-2291). Containing more than 800,000 acres, the park is larger than the state of Rhode Island, yet it's also one of the least visited parks in the country. Be prepared both for long, remote stretches without amenities, as well as some of the best motorcycling you will have ever encountered. Much of the Big Bend is **Chihuahuan Desert,** but the **Chisos Mountains,** located in the center of the park, rise to more than 7,000 feet in altitude. In the south, the Rio Grande River has cut deep canyons full of cane groves and rich vegetation. Many people spend weeks exploring this area and its natural beauty. The Indians say that when God was finished creating the world, he placed all the leftover rocks in the Big Bend. After your

This old movie set provides an interesting stop where you can still stroll "the Streets of Laredo." (photo by Jack Binion)

visit, you may be a believer. Note that the rich wildlife of the area is not all friendly toward man: bears, mountain lions, rattlesnakes, huge spiders, and scorpions all call the Big Bend home.

Day 4   Exploring the River Roads

Distance   *104 miles (54 paved, 50 dirt)*

Features   *If you have a dual-sport bike, you'll want to take an optional day to explore the hinterlands. Big Bend offers some excellent opportunities to get out into the backcountry. Off-road riding is not allowed, but a series of great dirt roads await you. This is a full day's ride, so plan accordingly.*

None of the unpaved roads in the Big Bend are technically difficult, but they would be best enjoyed with a dual-sport bike. Check with the local ranger station before heading out to learn about current hazards and weather conditions. Be sure to carry plenty of water, and make sure someone knows your route and when you plan to return. If you should encounter problems, your best bet will be to stay with your bike and wait for someone to come along—usually it will be only an hour or two. Unless you are sure that you are near the end of one of these roads, do not try to walk out. As always with dual-sport riding, a partner is recommended.

Leaving the Chisos Basin, return to the main road and turn left. After about 10 miles, turn left toward Santa Elena Canyon and retrace your route of the previous day until just before the village of Castolon (approx. 20 miles) where the left turn onto dirt is clearly marked as the **River Road**

This rider sure has come to the right place to test his dual-sport skills.

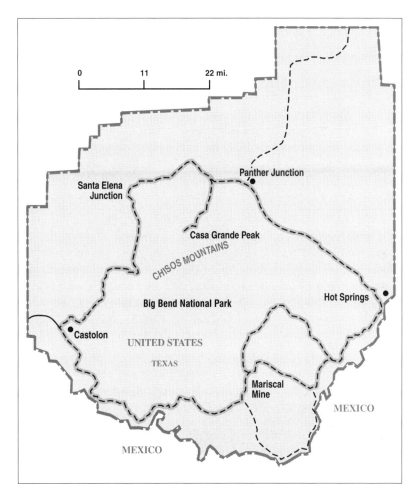

West. You will then begin a 50-mile ride that will really put you into the heart of Big Bend.

After 30 miles, it is very important that you take the right turn toward the **Mariscal Mine.** Seven miles after that, take the left turn on River Road. East to Hot Springs and Rio Grande Village. If you miss these turns, you will end up on some unmaintained roads that can really test your abilities. Should you feel up to it, try going straight at the Mariscal Mine turn off onto Black Gap Road. After 9 miles of this road, most folks will welcome the right turn to reconnect with the River Road East. When you hit pavement again, turn left and return to the Chisos Basin for a shower and bed.

These backroads offer so many opportunities for stops and side trips that it is almost impossible to list them all. If you want to explore, I suggest you purchase the *Road Guide to Backcountry Dirt Roads of Big Bend National Park,* available at the park headquarters. Throughout the area, be on the lookout for **mountain lions, bobcat, deer,** and **wild pigs.** Most of the wildlife is very shy and you will have to be very observant to spot one of these animals. Rattlesnakes, however, should be given a wide berth.

After about six miles on dirt, you will reach a highpoint that allows a wonderful view of the **Santa Elena Canyon,** thirteen miles in the distance. Stop, take your picture and enjoy the loneliness. Another nine miles will bring you to the ruins of the **Johnson Ranch.** This is the largest set of ruins in the park and a visit to the graveyard will lead most to think of the people who lived their entire lives in this remote area. There are several campsites along the road; permits are available at the ranger station.

Twenty-seven miles after entering the dirt, you will encounter some of the most difficult riding. Hang in there. This stretch only lasts for a few short miles. Also at about twenty-seven miles, you will find the turn off to the **Talley Ranch.** This six-mile side trip will take you to the Rio Grande, the ruins of the Talley Ranch and a favorite camping spot for many.

After thirty-two miles of dirt, you will reach the **Mariscal Mine,** the site of a mercury mine that existed from 1900 until 1923. Today we are warned about handling any of the dirt or other things in the area due to the possibility of mercury poisoning. One can only wonder what the Mexican laborers at this mine endured. Continue through this beautiful, but harsh, desert until you find pavement just north of **Rio Grande Village.**

You should be careful when encountering a javelina (wild pig) as they can turn nasty when annoyed. (photo by Bill Reeves/TxDOT)

Campers feel like they are in heaven when camping in the Big Bend Park. (photo by Richard Reynolds/TxDOT)

Day 5   Big Bend to Marfa

Distance *160 miles (via pavement), 150 miles (via the alternate route)*

Features *Today, you will be exploring the eastern side of Big Bend, either via dirt or pavement. The historic Gage hotel in Marathon is worth a stop. Wide-open spaces, wild-west towns, and wonderful people will make this a day to remember.*

From Chisos Basin, return to the main road and turn right toward Panther Junction. From Panther Junction it is only twenty miles to the village of Rio Grande, which consists of a gas station and snack store. But even without a great road in, two things make it worth the trip: the hot springs and the over-look at Baquillas Canyon.

The well-marked right turn to the **hot springs** will take you down a two-mile side road. The naturally occurring **hot springs** are only a short walk down a well-maintained trail and there are almost always others around en-joying the spot. Bring you bathing suit. After a good soak, you should then continue on the main road through the tunnel to the left turn toward

The hot springs in the Big Bend National Park offer a refreshing stop for all. (photo by Jack Binion)

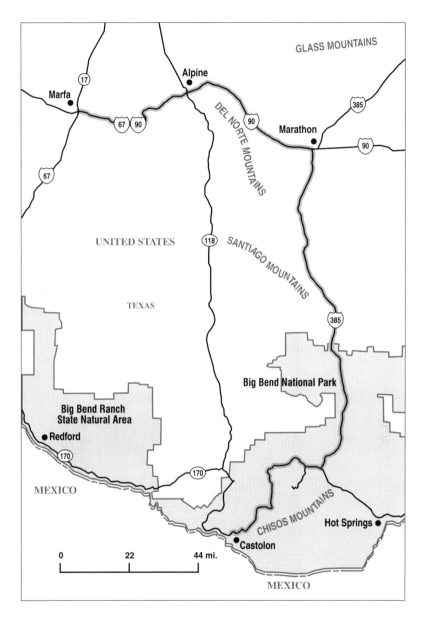

Baquillas, at the eastern end of **Big Bend National Park.** It is possible to cross the Rio Grande into Mexico via a small boat, but there really is not much on the Mexican side, unless you want a beer. Backtrack to Panther Junction and take Hwy. 385 north toward Marathon.

✪ *Dual-Sport Option*

On your return from Baquillas, turn right just past the tunnel onto the old Ore Road for 26 miles, then turn left on the Dagger Flat Road for two miles, and you will reconnect with pavement near the **Persimmon Gap** entrance at the north end of the park. Ore Road was the main road for hauling ore to Marathon and this route has quite a change in elevation. Several abandoned ranch houses and mining ruins are along this road, usually located near springs (identified by lush flora and in one case, old water tanks). Note that this dirt road is not for the faint-hearted; a lot of sand sits in the washes. But it's fun!

After exiting the park, continue on Hwy. 385. In forty miles, at the junction with Hwy. 90 at Marathon, turn left toward Marfa. This road, though

Large rock mountains seem to just jump up from the west Texas desert. (courtesy of Pancho Villa Moto-Tours)

Should your schedule permit, an overnight at the Gage Hotel in Marathon is a treat. (photo by Jack Binion)

flat and straight, leads you through the **Santiago** and **Woods Hollow Mountains** and makes for a great ride. Keep your eye out for low-flying **Air Force planes** practicing maneuvers.

Marathon (pop. 800) is a typical small, west Texas town in that it has most of the services needed for survival, but little else. The crowing jewel in Marathon is the **Gage Hotel,** built in 1927 by **Alfred Gage,** a rancher that once had a 500,000-acre ranch in the area and needed a place to house his frequent guests and visiting business associates. It was renovated in 1978 and is decorated and furnished in period fashion. While all the rooms feature a 1920s west Texas ranch decor, they are all different. Rooms range from "basic" (bath down the hall), to "nice" (bath in the room), to "wonderful" (private suites with fireplaces). It is a fairly expensive place with rates from $70 and up, but it is worth stopping just to look around.

Fifty-five miles on Hwy. 90 from Marathon, will get you to Marfa. About eight miles before arriving in Marfa, note the **pull-off area on the left** from

No one has ever solved the riddle of the mysterious Marfa Lights.

which you can view the Marfa Lights, as you may wish to return here at night.

As you ride into the town of **Marfa** (pop. 2,500), you will see that the "lights" are the big attraction here and many of the buildings and souvenir shops sport an alien theme. Marfa also contains a beautiful courthouse constructed from local stone in 1886. Atop the courthouse dome stands a life-sized statue of Lady Justice, though she is missing her scales. A local man who felt that he had not received justice inside, reportedly shot them off upon departing. The movie *Giant* was filmed in Marfa, and the lobby of the **El Paisano Hotel** on 207 N. Highland Avenue ($100+; 915-729-3145) displays some of the memorabilia from the film. **The Holiday Capri Inn** ($50;

915-729-4391), located on your left as you go into town on Hwy. 90, is a more than adequate place to stay with a decent café next door. There are no campsites available in Marfa or nearby.

The **Marfa Lights** are an enigma. They are most often referred to as "those mysterious Marfa Lights." These bright orbs were first noticed by settlers in the late 1800s. They appear, disappear, separate into multiple lights, change color, and move around throughout the year, but are seen most frequently in the fall. Scientists who have studied them for years still have no explanation for them. Perhaps you can figure it out. The locals love their lights and they are one of west Texas' top tourist attractions. Be very careful riding to and from the viewing area, as there is much wildlife along the road at night here.

Day 6   Marfa to Whites City, New Mexico

Distance *175 miles*

Features *This will be a day of mostly wide-open riding on flat, straight roads with wonderful views of mountains in the distance. Even though it gets curvier as you climb over the Guadalupe Mountains, it is still high-speed riding. Plan to stop at Carlsbad Caverns National Park in the afternoon.*

Ride west on Hwy. 90 for approximately 73 miles to Van Horn, then take Hwy. 54 north for 55 miles to the intersection with Hwys. 180/62 (straight ahead).

Guadalupe National Park is one of the newest of our national parks, created in 1972, and it receives fewer than 300,000 visitors each year, many of whom come in the fall to see the leaves turn. **Guadalupe Mountain,** at over 8,700 feet in altitude, is the highest point in Texas. The park headquarters, on the left on Hwy. 180/62, offers several exhibits outlining what lives and grows in the park. Rangers are available to answer your questions. There are no lodgings or eating facilities, but camping is allowed on a first-come-first-served basis. As you exit the park to the north, a nice "mom and pop" café, **The Nickel,** has a limited, yet delicious, menu.

From this point, continue on Hwy. 180/62 to **Whites City,** a town that exists solely because it is close to Carlsbad Caverns National Park. In Whites City, there are three **Best Western** motels ($80; 800-CAVERNS) on the highway at the intersection with the turn leading to Carlsbad Caverns. They are grouped around a "turn of the west" type strip mall that contains two restaurants, a souvenir shop, grocery store, small museum and a self-styled "opera house" with live entertainment. Camping in a large grassy area is available within walking distance of all facilities. All campsites have grills, restrooms, and showers on site. A larger range of motel options and prices exist only 16 miles further up the road in Carlsbad, the city.

Carlsbad Caverns are a series of eighty caves covering more than 73 square miles of labyrinths. Exploration continues to chart new caves. It is believed to be the largest such underground complex in the world. The main cavern is over 30 miles long.

Self-guided tours range from easy to moderately difficult and typically take anywhere from an hour or two, or longer; ranger-guided tours can last all day. To get a taste, take the elevator down and stroll along one of the many well-lit trails through the **Great Room,** which is more than 2 million

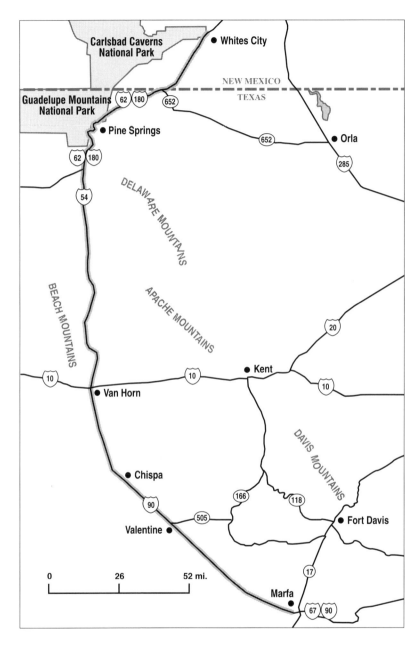

square feet in size. There is even a snack bar and seating area down there! Every night at dusk during the summer, **thousands of bats** exit the caves for their nightly feeding. A viewing area provides "the best seat in the house" from which to watch them fly.

Day 7   Whites City of El Paso via Cloudcroft, New Mexico

Distance *281 miles*

Features *This day starts in open desert and continues on to some absolutely knock-your-socks-off mountain roads and views. A thrilling decent of more than 4,300 feet in a short 16 miles drops you back to the flat desert. Leaving the forests, you can see the famous White Sands of New Mexico as you make a straightforward run to El Paso. Make sure you get an early start!*

From Whites City, turn left and continue north 22 miles on Hwy. 62/180 to Carlsbad. At the intersection with Hwy. 285 in Carlsbad, turn left toward Artesia. Between Carlsbad and Artesia you will notice a **strong odor in the air** created from the gasses associated with the production of crude oil. In Texas this is called the smell of money!

After approximately 34 miles, you will arrive in Artesia. Turn left (west) onto Hwy. 82 toward Cloudcroft. After 48 miles, turn left onto Hwy. 24 and continue 26 miles to the small town of Pinion. All these flat, straight roads through the high desert are reminiscent of the movie *High Plains Drifter*. From here, get ready for some superior mountain riding.

The Weed Cafe in Weed, New Mexico, offers good food and friendly people, where you can catch up on the local gossip. (photo by Jack Binion)

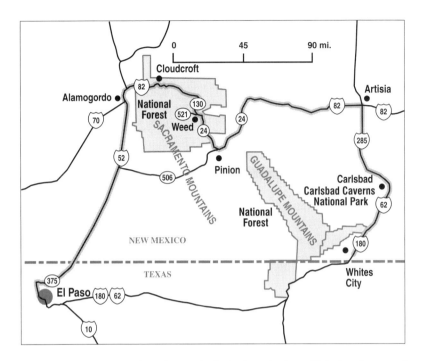

From Pinion, Hwy. 24 twists and climbs into the beautiful pine forests of the **Sacramento Mountains.** After roughly 22 miles, Hwy. 521 goes to the left into the town of Weed. If you want to meet some friendly people and have a good country lunch, try the **Weed Café** about 2 miles down Hwy. 521.

Two more miles down Hwy. 24, turn right onto Hwy. 130. Five miles later, turn left onto Hwy. 82. From here, the 18 miles to Cloudcroft will be a high point. Adjust your speed to suit your mood.

Cloudcroft (pop 600, elev. 8,950 ft.) was established when the **El Paso & Northeastern Railroad** built a spur from Alamagordo into the nearby Sacramento Mountains. Its purpose was to transport logs for railroad ties in their ambitious expansion northward. The spur, completed in 1900, showed the developers an area so beautiful that they decided to establish a resort for vacationers. Named Cloudcroft, a pasture for clouds, the resort was an instant success. Originally consisting of only a tent city, more permanent structures and private vacation homes were built gradually. Around 1947, when automobiles made railroads less profitable, the tracks were removed—but little has changed since then. Its population has remained relatively stable over the years and it offers all the services normally required by a visitor.

The rooms in the Cloudcroft Hotel are large enough for an old wood-burning stove.

Texas grass.

If you want to make a leisurely side trip to the White Sands National Monument, consider staying in Cloudcroft and getting a start in the morning. The **Cloudcroft Hotel** ($75; 505-682-3414) is located right on the square in the middle of town, with several dining options within walking distance. Try the **Western Bar and Grill** for breakfast! There are also five campgrounds within two miles of downtown, all with fire rings, toilet facilities, and water.

From Cloudcroft continue west on Hwy. 82. The 16-mile, snaking descent to Alamagordo will have your heart pumping—but the views make it hard to keep your eyes on the road. From Alamagordo, you will be about 90 miles from El Paso on Hwy. 54.

✪ *Side Trip*

A visit to the **White Sands National Monument,** with its towering dunes of gypsum, can be quite a unique experience. The 16-mile scenic route has several well-marked pull-offs with interpretive signs explaining what you are seeing. Surrounded by the White Sands missile range, the park is sometimes closed for an hour or so when testing is in progress. To get there, turn right in Alamagordo onto Hwy. 70 (west). Fifteen miles later, you will see the park entrance and visitors' center on your right. As I mentioned, for a leisurely visit, consider staying in Cloudcroft and getting a start in the morning.

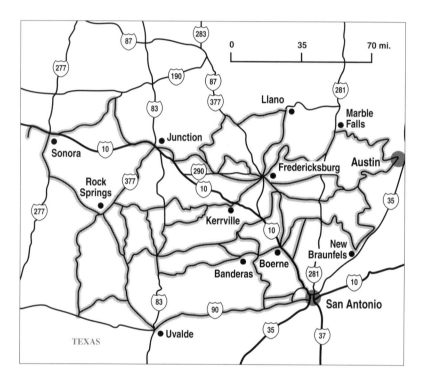

San Antonio The Hill Country

The loosely defined area known as the Hill Country covers more than twenty thousand square miles of land atop the Balcones Escarpment in the "heart" of Texas. Although altitudes typically range only 1,500–1,700 ft., the dry air of summer and temperatures that are relatively mild compared to the surrounding cities attract many visitors trying to escape the heat—and it offers all sorts of outdoor activities—including great motorcycling.

Located around Austin and San Antonio, the Hill Country is sprinkled with many small towns. Only few of which can boast populations exceeding 10,000. Almost all government buildings and many homes and motels are built with the locally available pink limestone. Settled mostly by Europeans of German, Czech, and Polish descent, it retains much of that heritage to this day with many restaurants and cafés specializing in good food reflecting these roots.

The Hill Country presents a rider with endless options of up-and-down, curving, twisting roads. Many, of which, trail along rivers or atop high ridgelines with tremendous views of the countryside. When any roads in these routes are described as a "typical" Hill Country road, read this to mean that you are in for yet another fabulous motorcycle ride. After years, even locals report that they are still discovering superb new routes in this wonderfully interconnected "spaghetti bowl" of bike roads. DeLorme's *Texas Atlas & Gazetteer* has very detailed maps of the area and very helpful in navigating these smaller, less traveled roads.

The Hill Country can be quite hot in the summer—cool by Texas standards, of course, but still hot by most standards. During the mild winters, temperatures rarely fall below freezing at night and generally hover in the 60s or 70s during the day. The spring months of April and May carpet the Hill Country in bluebonnets, Indian paintbrush, and other wildflowers, to create a sight right out of a Monet painting.

This chapter outlines five day rides with a home base in **Fredericksburg,** which is about a day's ride from San Antonio. Three routes are day rides from **Rocksprings,** one is a day loop starting and ending in **San Antonio,** with connecting routes between the two base towns. Please consider the rides outlined herein as only a brief introduction to what is available. Heck,

San Antonio is worth a few days by itself, and I'd encourage you to allow some extra time for exploring this beautiful city on your own.

A visit to the **Alamo** is a must, as is a stroll down **The Riverwalk** to have a delightful meal under the overhanging trees. The restaurants along this walk can provide any kind of food known in the world—except cheap food. A boat ride down the **San Antonio River** will let you survey the dining and shopping, while eyeballing the other tourists eyeballing you.

Remember, even with a population of more than 1.1 million, San Antonio consistently ranks in travel magazines as **one of the ten best places to visit** in the United States. *Conde Nast* has even rated it one of the top ten destinations in the world. It is the number one tourist draw in Texas. And that's saying something.

But don't think that you will be crowded among all the visitors. San Antonio is plenty big enough. Soon the laid-back, local, *mañana* pace will be rubbing off on you, and a good time will be had by all.

San Antonio's varied economy is grounded in the five U.S. military bases that exist in the city. The oldest, **Fort Sam Houston,** dates back to 1876. The federal government pours billions of dollars into the local economy in the form of paychecks for the troops and creates thousands of jobs to support their needs and desires. Tourism, the number two influence on the economy, funnels untold "outside" dollars through the local service industry. Bioscience and high-tech industries also thrive here, and there are eleven universities within the city limits. Being Texas, the oil business also contributes toward the growing and energetic economy.

As you would expect, San Antonio has many world-class museums and a multitude of cultural activities. The **San Antonio Convention and Visitors Bureau,** located at 317 Alamo Plaza, is happy to direct you on the many interesting things to see and do here. You can also call (800-447-3372) or visit their website (www.sanantoniocvb.com).

The **Alamo** (on Alamo Street between E. Houston and E. Crockett) is a former Spanish presidio that was constructed in 1724 and originally named the **Misión San Antonio de Valero.** It served as a home and workplace for the Spanish padres as they tried to convert the Indians. In 1793 the government took over the mission and expanded it into a true fort.

The Alamo is dear to the hearts of all Texans for the role it played in the fight for independence from Mexico in 1836. During the famous battle, 189 Texicans and other adventurers, most notably **Davy Crockett** and **Jim Bowie,** held off a Mexican army of more than 5,000 led by **General Santa Anna** for thirteen days before they were overrun and killed to the man. While the actual details of, and the motivation for, the battle remain fuzzy to

In the hearts and minds of most Texans, the Alamo is one of the most sacred spots on this earth. (photo by Richard Reynolds/TxDOT)

this day, it is true that the delaying of the Mexican army at the Alamo allowed time for other Texicans to gather and form up into the military force that ultimately defeated the Mexicans at **San Jacinto.** It gave the Texicans their rallying battle cry, "Remember the Alamo!"

After the Texas War of Independence, the Alamo served various functions, and was even abandoned for a time. In 1903 the Daughters of the Republic of Texas (women who are descended from the defenders of the Alamo) took over this property, restored it, and operate it to this day. A self-guided walking tour is available throughout the complex and a 30-minute guided tour is given several times a day. There are also slide shows and a short film that detail the story of the battle and the history of the site itself.

These days, some controversy exists regarding the historical presentation of the battle, claiming it is too one-sided and does not reflect fairly the Mexican viewpoint. Be assured, you will leave with no doubts as to the Texican side of things!

There is ample parking near the Alamo, primarily in hotel parking garages. As a side note, Texas law expressly forbids one from urinating on the Alamo. After being caught for a dastardly infraction, singer **Ozzy Osborne** has been permanently banned from performing in the state—Texas justice.

The **Riverwalk** is San Antonio's second most popular tourist attraction and should not be missed. You can enter the riverwalk within two blocks of the Alamo and do not need to move your bike. The **San Antonio River** originally ran right through downtown. In 1921 it flooded, destroying homes and businesses, and killing more than fifty people. This resulted in the construction of a dam, and the **Oxbow Canal** was built to handle future floods. It was planned that the original river course would be covered over, as a massive drainage system. Some farsighted business leaders, however, suggested that the river could be a pleasant stroll for locals and visitors to enjoy.

Progress on the project was slow until the WPA took over in 1938, installing cobbled walkways, attractive stonewalls, and many entranceways to create a beautiful setting. Despite this, the Riverwalk was not an instant success. In fact, it became somewhat of an eyesore and a health hazard due to water pollution. The area became rampant with crime.

In 1946 the first restaurant was built along the walk and soon boats were being rented for rides. The area boomed in 1968 when the **World's Fair** (HemisFair) came to town. Construction along the river produced many businesses and hotels, and the city made a major effort to make the area safe. Today the riverwalk is dotted with pleasant restaurants, shops, and major hotels. It is also safe. The city appreciates its value in tourist dollars and police presence is everywhere. Spend an hour or two strolling, take a boat ride and enjoy a meal along the Riverwalk.

In addition to the Alamo, the Spanish established four other missions along the San Antonio River in the 1700s: Missions Concepción, San José,

The San Antonio Riverwalk is a great place to shop, walk, or enjoy an excellent meal outdoors.

This is just one of four reasons you will want to ride the Mission Trail in San Antonio. (photo by Jack Lewis/TxDOT)

San Juan, and Espada. At **San Antonio Missions National Historical Park** you can visit these missions, all of which still serve as active Catholic churches along the **Mission Trail**— an 8-mile ride clearly marked by Mission Trail signs. From the Alamo, go south on S. Alamo, pick up trail signs, and go left onto South St. Mary's Street. Each of the missions has a unique history and varies greatly in size and style. If you only have time to visit one, I recommend the **Mission San José,** which also serves as park headquarters and offers a free film that outlines the history of the missions and the Indian tribes who built them.

San Antonio offers lodgings in every price range and category. If you want a real treat, and your budget can handle it, try the **Menger Hotel** ($150; 800-345-9285). It is literally "in the shade" of the Alamo. Originally built in 1859, the hotel has been constantly renovated and updated through the years, yet maintains its original look. The staff and owners, well aware of the hotel's historical significance, are constantly on the lookout for any encroachment on its appearance.

The closest campground to downtown is the **Dixie Kampground,** located at 1011 Gembler Road ($14; 210-337-6502; 800-759-5627). Three miles east of downtown off I-35, take the Coliseum Exit and go south one half-mile to Gembler and follow signs. They have nice shaded camping sites with all facilities and a camp store. Ask about buses into town if you'd rather not worry about navigating and parking your bike.

Day 8   San Antonio to Fredericksburg

Distance *125 miles*

Features *This short ride will get you out of the traffic of the big city and give you an introduction to Hill Country. Fredericksburg makes a great home base for the next four loops. Please do not be fooled by the low mileage; a good bit of this day consists of very slow speed roads.*

From the intersection of I-10 and Loop 410 on the northwest side of San Antonio (near the airport), take 410 W for approximately 11 miles and then take the Hwy. 3487 Exit (Culbera Road). After a mile or so on this frontage road, take a right onto the actual highway at the first traffic signal. A block later, turn left onto Hwy. 1957.

After you cross the intersection with Loop 1604, Hwy. 1957 becomes two-lane and you will have exited the city. Eight miles after leaving the interstate you will come to a T-intersection with Hwy. 471; take a right and go 10 miles, then take a left onto Hwy. 1283. Hwy. 471 runs through flat farming land, but for some reason, the road has several 90-degree turns—not all marked—although you will have excellent visibility through the turns.

Named after its builder, Polly's Chapel sits alone in a remote area. Services are still held here.

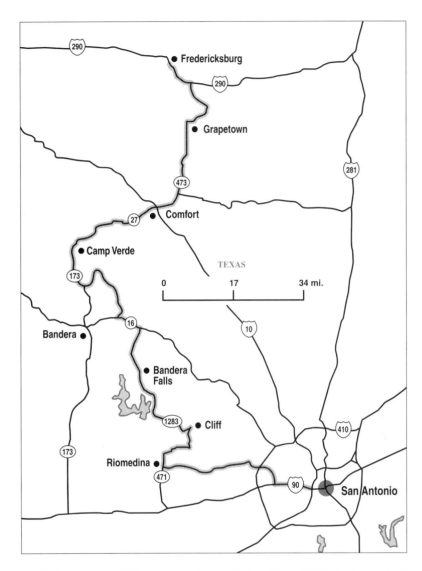

Welcome to the Hill Country! As you follow Hwy. 1283 for the next 22 miles to the intersection with Hwy. 16 in Pipe Creek you will get an idea of what is ahead of you on the trip. In spite of the high-speed designation of the road before you, you will get some wonderful views as you top hill after hill, and twist through the curves.

At the T-intersection with Hwy. 16 in the town of Pipe Creek, turn left, continue for approximately 4 miles, and turn right onto Privilege Creek Road. After two miles, the road turns to good, hard-packed dirt for about 8

A visit to this roadhouse in Fredericksburg is almost a "must" for some riders.

miles. Go left at the first Y-intersection onto Old School Road, toward Polly's Chapel. As you run along the river with cliffs on either side, note that the speed limit for this stretch is posted as 30 mph.

❍ *Side Trip*

Shortly after taking the turn onto Old School Road, you pass over a cattle guard and a right turn takes off toward **Polly's Chapel,** maybe a quarter of a mile away. Sitting out by itself on a small hill surrounded by live oak trees, Polly's Chapel was built by hand out of native stone in 1882 by **Policarpo Rodriguez,** a former Texas Ranger, army scout, and guide. It was here that he converted to the Methodist religion and services are still being held there today.

I recommend you take this small side trip, but note that there are about 20 yards of this road that require caution on a street bike. After visiting Polly's Chapel, return the short distance to the main road and turn right.

Continue on Old School Road for approximately 3 miles until you come to a Y-intersection, where you will bear left. After another 2 miles, you come to another Y-intersection. Take the right hand fork. In just 2 more miles, the road T's into pavement, where you will turn right. You soon come to another Y-intersection; take the right fork. In 2 more miles, at an intersection with a yield sign, proceed straight ahead. Six miles later you will be at a T-intersection, where you will turn right onto Hwy. 173.

After about 7 miles of good, high-speed riding on Hwy. 173, turn right onto Hwy. 480. Another 7 miles will get you to the intersection with Hwy. 27, where you should turn right again, and after 9 miles you will come into the small town of Comfort.

From Comfort you have two options for reaching Fredericksburg. The most direct and fastest route is to turn left onto Hwy. 87, and after approximately 23 miles of good road, you will be there. Your other choice is somewhat longer, consists of much better riding roads, and is more fun. To take this option, turn left onto Hwy. 473 in Comfort and head toward Sisterdale. After 5 miles, Hwy. 473 bears off to the right; stay left and follow signs indicating the **Old Tunnel Wildlife Management Area.** This ride is an absolute delight and has some serious curves on it that are not always clearly marked. Take extra care and enjoy! The Old Tunnel Wildlife Management Area was created to protect the many animals that live here. From June through October, the old railroad tunnel is home to over 1 million bats and their departure at sunset is an amazing sight.

Fourteen miles after leaving Hwy. 473, turn right onto Luckenbach-Cane City Road. Be alert. This turn is only marked by a very small sign. After 2 miles, turn left onto Hwy. 1376, go 5 miles, and turn left at the T-intersection with Hwy. 290. Nine miles later you will arrive in Fredericksburg. For more detail of the road between Comfort and Fredericksburg, see Day 11.

The people of the Hill Country are proud of their heritage and are constantly showing it off.

If you like good, authentic German food served by beautiful waitresses, you will have endless options in the Hill Country. (courtesy of TxDOT)

Fredericksburg, (pop. 8,000) is considered by many to be the center of the Hill Country. People flock here year 'round on day trips from San Antonio and Austin or for overnight stays during the spring when the wildflowers are in bloom. It can become crowded on weekends during this time and, if possible, plan your visit for weekdays.

Settled by German immigrants in 1846, Fredericksburg wears its heritage proudly. German is still the primary language of many residents, and the downtown architecture also pays homage to its roots. Fredericksburg also holds a unique footnote in history: its original German settlers entered into **a treaty with the local Comanche Indians** that was never broken, the only such treaty between white men and Native American to hold such a distinction. Fredericksburg was also the birthplace of **Admiral Chester Nimitz,** and a very good museum covering World War II in the Pacific and the life of the Admiral is located at 328 E. Main St, in a building that was the site of the old Nimitz Hotel. There are several rooms restored to that era for viewing. Ask at the front desk about the current times and starting locations for walking tours of the town.

The number one place to stay is the **Best Western Sunday House Inn** located at 501 E. Main Street ($70; 830-997-3344). It includes a free breakfast coupon redeemable at the **Sunday House Restaurant** next door. Another choice is the **Dietzel Motel** ($55; 830-997-3330), located about one mile west of downtown on Hwy. 290, just after Hwy. 87 goes to the right. Located next door to Friedlhelm's Bavärian Restaurant & Bar, this place is perfectly adequate. The ever-popular **Skookers Roadhouse,** a local biker hangout, is just around the corner on Hwy. 87. Fredericksburg also seems to have an endless supply of B&Bs (830-997-4712). Campers can set up along the **Pedernales River** at the **Lady Bird Johnson Municipal Park** ($7) just south of town.

The problem with the food in Fredericksburg is that there are so many good places to eat it is hard to choose. Most tourists leave after their visit a few pounds heavier. I recommend **Das Lindenbaum** (with attached *biergarten)* at 312 E. Main and **Friedhelm's Bavärian Restaurant & Bar** at 905 W. Main. Great southwestern and Cajun dishes are served at the **Navajo Grill** at 209 E. Main, and the all-around pub menu at the **Fredericksburg Brewing Co.** at 245 E. Main has something for everyone. Of the many good German pastry shops in town, try **Dietz Bakery** or the **Fredericksburg Bakery,** both on E. Main Street.

Day 9   Fredericksburg to Austin (NE Loop)

Distance *225 miles*

Features *This ride contains two of the most talked-about roads in the Hill Country: Willow City Loop and Lime Creek Road. Visit the historic city of Austin and the LBJ ranch, and check out the views of the massive lake system north of Austin.*

In Fredericksburg take Hwy. 16 north for 20 miles and make a right turn onto Willow City Loop Road. Highway 16 is a good high-speed road with a fair amount of traffic for the Hill Country. Willow City Loop Road is one of the many one-lane, two-way roads you will find in this area, and it bounces up and down, twisting and turning through the countryside for all of its 13 miles. You should stay alert for oncoming traffic, keep a sharp eye for live-stock out on the open range, and look for sand or gravel washes in the dips. Slow down and enjoy the ride.

As you come through Willow City, proceed straight ahead at the intersection with Rural Road 1323. After 18 miles of some of best riding to be found anywhere, you will arrive in the one-store town of **Sandy.** Be extra careful along this stretch as it does have some extreme dips and a few tight curves that can sneak up on you if you are not paying attention. Clearing through the traffic and congestion of Sandy, take the first paved left onto Sandy/Round Mountain Road, which quickly turns to good hard-packed dirt for 8 miles through the countryside before intersecting with Hwy. 281 just north of Johnson City.

> ○ *Alternate Route*
>
> If you do not wish to ride the dirt section, continue on Rural Road 1323 until it intersects with Hwy. 281 where you turn left toward Marble Falls. About 13 miles from Marble Falls, you rejoin the rec-ommended route.

At the end of the Sandy/Round Mountain Road turn left at the T-intersection with Hwy. 281. Thirteen good, high-speed miles later you will cross the river and enter the town of **Marble Falls.** At the top of the hill on your right is the **Bluebonnet Café,** famous for its down-home cooking and deserts. Try to arrive hungry!

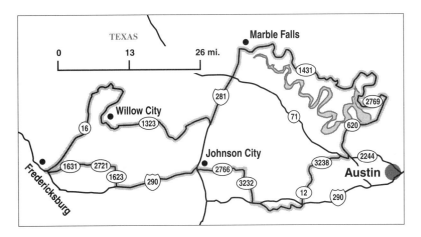

In Marble Falls, take a right onto Rural Road 1431. Go 39 miles and turn right onto Lime Creek Road, a stretch that passes through several small towns and offers magnificent views of the rivers and lakes that make up this part of the Hill Country. As you approach the outskirts of Austin, the road becomes a four-laner.

✪ Side Trip

Austin once served as the **national capitol** of the Republic of Texas; it was demoted to a mere state capitol when Texas joined the Union. Should you wish to visit this delightful city, continue on Hwy. 1431 past the Lime Creek Road turnoff to the T-intersection with Hwy. 183, where you should take a right. Follow Hwy. 183 to the intersection with I-35 and go south.

You will find hotels to fit every taste and budget along this route. For a real treat, try staying at the **Driskell Hotel** ($170; 512-474-5911) located at 604 Brazos Street. Constructed in 1886, the building served as a meeting place for the Texas government until the capitol was completed. Built to the highest standards of the day, the hotel retains it original décor while having all the modern amenities.

Austin (metro area pop. 1,000,000+) has been picked as **one of the top five places to live** in the United States by both *Money* and *Fortune* magazines. The government of Texas and its employees form a large part of the city. The more than 50,000 students of the **University of Texas** also make up a large part of the local culture. And lastly, the electronics industry has contributed to the city's economic health: today, Austin is the home of Texas Instruments, Dell

The Governor's Mansion in Austin reflects the influence of the South in Texas.
(photo by Gay Shackelford/TxDOT)

Computer, IBM, Hewlett-Packard, Apple Computer and more than 200 other high-tech companies, and is often referred to as the **Silicon Valley of the East.** As a result of the above, the people of Austin are the most highly educated of any city in the United States, with one-third holding college degrees.

In addition, Austin is a major record recording center to rival Nashville with its country music and Memphis with its blues. Whatever your taste in music, you'll have your choice of nightclubs with live entertainment every night of the week. While Austin is a major city with museums, art galleries, and cultural opportunities to match any other major city in the world, it does have some unique sites of its own.

The **state capitol building,** completed in 1888, is the largest state capitol in the nation and is even seven feet taller than the U.S. Capitol in Washington, D.C. Its exterior consists of pink limestone mined at Marble Falls only a few miles away. The more than eight acres of interior floor space are covered with a copper dome that is topped by a statue of the Goddess of Liberty. The rotunda, which houses the original **Texas Declaration of Independence** and the **Ordinance of Secession,** has a terrazzo floor featuring the flags of the six nations that have, at one time or another, claimed dominion over Texas: Spain,

France, Mexico, the Republic of Texas, the Confederate States of America and the United States. Take a free, guided tour that includes the governor's offices and the chambers of the state senate and the house of representatives—just brace yourself to be bombarded by "Texas-sized" statistics!

By itself, the **Congress Avenue Bridge** is not much of an attraction, but during the summer, an estimated 1.5 million Mexican bats call the place "home." The bats migrate and nest here from May through October, and their daily sunset exodus into the night sky is an amazing sight. Volunteers from **Bat Conservation International** are on duty to answer questions, or you can call the bat hotline (512-416-5700, ext. 3636) for information.

Austin is the center of the fourteen campuses that make up the vast **University of Texas** system, which consistently ranks among the top ten schools in the nation. Sitting on a 357-acre site in downtown Austin, UTexas is the home of more than 50,000 students; it is so large, one residence hall has its own zip code. The university library is the sixth-largest in the country, with more than six million volumes. The endowment of the University of Texas is one of the largest in the world, due to the fact that the state legislature gave the school more than two million acres of land in the west Texas desert, which were later discovered to contain vast oilfields. (It's no coincidence that the Petroleum Engineering Dept. is world class!)

There are several museums on the campus, but the most popular tourist spot is the **UT Tower** from which, in August 1966, **Charles Whitman** shot and killed 15 people and wounded 33 more before being shot to death himself. The second most visited spot is the **Lyndon B. Johnson Library and Museum** which contains four floors of memorabilia and a replica of the Oval Office during his terms as president.

For everything you ever wanted to know about Texas history, visit the state-of-the-art **Bob Bullock Texas State History Museum,** located at the corner of MLK Blvd. and Congress Avenue. Don't miss the **Texas Spirit Theater** showing of the film *Star of Destiny,* a Hollywood-class production that will have you charging into the streets screaming, "Remember the Alamo!" Plan on spending at least a half day here, enjoying the hands-on, interactive exhibits. Underground parking is available.

A series of dams near Austin have created beautiful lakes surrounded by upscale housing developments.

Lime Creek Road runs for 11 miles along the lake, and it appears no attempts were made to grade or straighten when it was built, as it clings to the hillsides and meanders along. At the STOP sign turn left onto Rural Road 2769, go 7 miles, and make a right turn onto Hwy. 620, which runs along the lakefront where there are many gated communities of million-dollar homes. This road also has several very sharp curves with recommended speeds of 15 to 25 mph. Believe the signs!

After 18 miles on Hwy. 620, turn right on Hwy. 71 in Bee Cave; three miles later, take a left onto Rural Road 3238. After 5 miles, turn left onto Hwy. 12 toward Dripping Springs. You will have left behind the build-up surrounding Austin, as Hwy. 12 runs along a ridgeline almost its entire length. After 5 miles, turn right onto Hwy. 290, and follow the four-lane main road for only a short distance, maybe two blocks, and take a left onto

Creek Road. It is easy to miss this turn; the road is directly across from the signs indicating Loop 64 off to right.

Creek Road soon becomes a one-lane, two-way road, with several one-lane bridges along its nine-mile path. Three miles after the turnoff from Hwy. 290, turn right at the intersection with County Road 220 to continue on Creek Road. At the T-intersection with Hwy. 165, turn right, and then at the T-intersection with Hwy. 290, take another left.

In approximately 3 miles, turn right onto Rural Road 3232 and proceed another 7 miles to the T-intersection with Rural Road 2766. Take a right, and then an almost immediate left at the signs denoting the entranceway into the **Pedernales Falls State Park.** As you might guess by the name, the park adjoins the **Pedernales River** and has a view of the falls. In the summer, this is a popular spot to launch canoes for a pristine paddle in the wilderness.

After visiting the park, return to Rural Road 2766 and turn right. Continue on this road for 12 miles and then turn right on Hwy. 290. After completing the run on Rural Road 2766, you may begin to wonder just how many excellent motorcycle roads exist in the Hill Country. Too many to count. Enjoy!

A block or so into Johnson City, turn left onto Hwy. 290, a high-speed, four-lane highway whose elevation affords overwhelming views. Fifteen miles later, the LBJ Ranch will be on your right. Officially known as the **Lyndon B. Johnson State and National Historical Parks,** the complex contains the ranch house that served as the "Texas Whitehouse" during Johnson's term as president, a reconstructed cabin which represents his boyhood home, an active visitors' center detailing his life and accomplishments, and the family graveyard where he is buried. A 90-minute bus tour points out the sights and explains what you are seeing. Note that this is no place for trotting out political opinions detrimental to the memory of the 36th president. To Texans, this is, after all, hallowed ground.

After your visit to the ranch complex, exit and continue on Hwy. 290 for about a mile and make a right turn on Rural Road 1623. After 4 miles take a left onto 2721, proceed to the intersection with Rural Road 1631, and go straight ahead. Thirteen miles later, turn right onto Hwy. 290 to downtown Fredericksburg.

Day 10   Fredericksburg to Mason (NW Loop)

Distance *165 miles*

Features *This ride affords a visit to Enchanted Rock State Park, a "must-stop" at Cooper's Bar-B-Q in Mason, opportunities to view exotic game, and a short dual-sport ride that includes three stream crossings.*

Enchanted Rock rises 325 feet above the surrounding terrain.

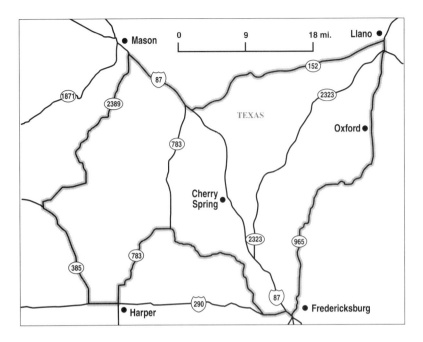

Start at the intersection of Hwy. 290/87 and Hwy. 16 in downtown Fredericksburg. Go north on Hwy. 290/87 for a few blocks. Make a right turn onto Rural Road 965 to begin another day of delightful Hill Country riding. After 17 miles, Enchanted Rock State Park will be on your left.

Enchanted Rock, a popular spot with rock climbers, juts up 325 ft. and covers more than 70 acres. The night air is filled with strange creaking and groaning sounds due to the contraction of the rocks as they cool each day. The Indians thought the place was haunted and it is believed they performed human sacrifices here to appease the gods. Even today, many people consider it a spiritual power point on Earth. You can ride down a short loop to get a closer view and take the obligatory picture of your bike in front of this amazing rock. A small welcome center has exhibits explaining more details.

Following your visit, continue northward on Rural Road 965 for nine miles. At the intersection with Hwy. 16, turn left toward Llano. After 15 miles of good, high-speed road make a left turn onto Hwy. 152. If you cross the bridge going into Llano you will have gone too far.

Hwy. 152 runs 20 miles until it intersects with Hwy. 87—and it is some of the best the Hill Country has to offer. Nine miles into this stretch, be on the lookout for the left turn just before the small town of Castell. Rather than scraping your pegs (which can easily be done), I suggest you slow down and savor this wonderful ride; there are several curves with recommended speed limits in the 15–20 mph range.

At the intersection with Hwy. 87, turn right toward Mason. After 11 miles on this major highway, turn left onto Rural Road 1723 (Jamestown Bat Cave Road).

✪ Side Trip

For a real Texas treat, continue into **Mason** just a few short blocks and let your nose lead you to **Cooper's Bar-B-Q.** You'll see the smoke rising before you actually see the building. Once you've sorted out all the delicious smells, proceed to the outdoor pits to choose the size and nature of your carnivorous feast. Your selection will be cut and placed on a piece of white waxed paper that will serve as your plate. From there, you go inside to have your order weighed and to stock up on sides of cold slaw, beans, and potato salad. Then, have a seat and pig out. Afterward, backtrack on Hwy. 16 for a mile or so and make a right turn onto Hwy. 1723.

Ten miles after turning onto Rural Road 1723, the road turns to dirt, and that 18-mile stretch includes three places where you have to ford the **James River.** It is very do-able and fun on a dual-sport bike, but I don't think it would be much fun on a heavy dresser.

✪ Alternate Route

If you decide to skip the dirt, continue through Mason and take a left onto Rural Road 1871. At the T-intersection with Hwy. 385, turn left and pick up the remainder of the route after passing E. Mill Road. This will add a few miles, but is quicker than the suggested route.

As you travel the 28 miles of road from Hwy. 87 to the intersection with Hwy. 365, you will really be in the backcountry. Keep your eyes peeled for wild turkey and deer. Those stretches of high fencing you see often seal-off **exotic animal ranches** with species imported from around the world.

Two miles after leaving State Hwy. 87, turn right onto Rural Road 2389, which turns to good, hard-packed dirt after another 8 miles. There are several intersections on the 10-mile paved stretch that can be confusing; just follow the signs to the bat cave. This road runs right along the banks of the James River and should be missed. Two miles after starting on the dirt, a paved road takes off to the right to a privately owned ranch; continue straight on the dirt. After 6 miles of dirt, you will come to the first of three water crossings along this road.

The first crossing is by far the longest and deepest (perhaps one-hundred yards of foot-deep water. Before starting across, note the barbed wire fence on the left: if the water is up to the lower strand, it's about 12 inches deep. The next two crossings are much shorter and only have an inch or two of water in them.

Shortly after passing the bat cave, make a right turn onto E. Mill Road. Another 7 miles of dirt will bring you to the T-intersection with Hwy. 385, where you turn left. Follow Hwy. 385 for 14 miles to the T-intersection with Hwy. 290. This ride is fairly straight with lots of gentle ups and downs. There are several exotic game ranches along this road, too.

Turn left onto Hwy. 290, go 3 miles, and turn left on Hwy. 783, which goes through a more settled area with farms and pastures on each side. Don't

While lacking in amenities, Cooper's Bar-B-Q in Mason does serve up some real Texas cooking.

A tall fences in the Hill Country might mean you could spot an exotic imported animal.

let this road lull you into a false sense of security, as there are several sharp curves that can sneak up on you. Fourteen miles later, turn right onto Doss Spring Creek Road, go a short 2 miles, and turn left onto Crenwelge Ridge Road. Six miles later, turn left onto Rehwienheiner Road, and proceed six miles to the T-intersection with Hwy. 290. The 24-mile loop from the time you leave Hwy. 290 until your return has a good many sections of one-lane, two-way traffic and lots of open range. It is a beautiful Hill Country ride; slow down and enjoy.

Turn left on Hwy. 290 and about nine miles later you will be back in Fredericksburg.

You might have to ford an occasional stream on the many backroads in the Hill Country.

Day 11   Fredericksburg to Luckenbach (SW Loop)

Distance *195 miles*

Features *The Lower Guadalupe Fork Road is one of the best and longest rides in the Hill Country. Visit the Cowboy Artists of America Museum in Kerrville and "gang up" with local riders.*

Starting at the intersection of HwySs. 290 and 16 in Fredericksburg, take Hwy. 16 south toward Kerrville. After 25 miles of good, high-speed road you will go under the interstate and enter Kerrville, with a very complete welcome center on your right, just across from the EconoLodge.

This weathered cowboy sure looks like he has seen better days, but he can still write and sing wonderful songs. (photo by Geoff Appold/TxDOT)

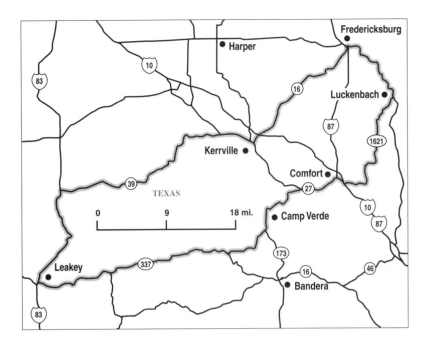

Kerrville (pop. 20,000) is a popular Hill Country getaway for hot city folks living in Austin and San Antonio. Tourism is the primary industry, and outdoor lovers flock here to ride horses, hike, and enjoy nature. The old downtown area has been restored to its original glory and now blooms with shops and sidewalk restaurants.

To get to the **Cowboy Artists of America Museum,** continue down Hwy. 16, cross the river, and turn left onto Hwy. 173. A half-mile later it will be on your right. The museum features historically accurate paintings and sculptures depicting the cowboy and his life. You will come away with a view that is very different from Hollywood's portrayal. After your visit to the museum, backtrack to the intersection with Hwy. 27 and turn left.

If you do not wish to visit the museum, turn right onto Hwy. 27 toward Ingram. After 6 miles of four-lane road, you will come to an intersection; go straight ahead to get onto Hwy. 39 (Lower Guadalupe Fork Rd). For the next 41 miles, the road runs along the banks of the **Guadalupe River,** following its turns through rocky, wooded country. You will cross the river a half-dozen times. The speed limit on this road is typically 50 mph, but the road flattens and straightens out the last 10 miles or so and the speed limit increases to 70 mph.

At the T-intersection with Hwy. 83, turn left toward Leakey. While this is a major highway, it does offer a stunning panoramic view of the countryside.

Rivers don't always have water, but when they do, they can become raging torrents.

There is a super pull-off about 10 miles down this road which is perfect for getting a shot of your noble beast in the Hill Country. Nine miles later on Hwy. 83, you will arrive in **Leakey.** For good country cooking and local gossip, try the **Frio Canyon Café.**

Continue south on Hwy. 83 for approximately 1 mile and make a left turn on Hwy. 337 toward Vanderpool. Again, this 17-mile stretch of Hill Country road will have you grinning from ear-to-ear and begging for more. As you approach Vanderpool, Hwy. 337 makes a 90-degree right as it joins with Hwy. 187, and then turns left just a short distance down the road; both turns are clearly marked.

Continue on Hwy. 337 for 18 miles. When you reach Hwy. 16 in Medina, turn right and go three miles. Turn left onto Rural Road 2828, proceed 9 miles, and turn left onto Hwy. 173. After 3 miles, turn right on Hwy. 480. Six miles later, at the intersection of Hwy. 27, turn right toward **Comfort.** This is a nice town with a historical district that is perfect for an interesting stroll or afternoon coffee-and-pastry break.

In Comfort, take a left turn onto Hwy. 473 toward Sisterdale, and follow the road signs to get through several intersections (just keep going straight). After 5 miles, Hwy. 473 will bear off to the right; go straight ahead following the signs indicating the Old Tunnel Wildlife Management Area. Local bikers know this as **"the Grapetown Rd,"** and it has some serious curves, not all of which are marked. It's an absolute delight.

The **Old Tunnel Wildlife Management Area** was created to protect the many animals that inhabit the area. From June through October, the old railroad tunnel is home to more than 1 million bats and their departure at sunset is an amazing sight; the show is even better with a full moon.

Fourteen miles after leaving Hwy. 473, turn right onto Luckenbach-Cane City Road. Be alert, as this turn is marked only by a very small sign. After 2 miles, turn right onto Hwy. 1376. Two miles farther, you will see the right turn into **Luckenbach.** If you cross the bridge, you have gone too far.

Founded as a German community in the 1800s, the entire town of Luckenbach (pop. 10) was purchased by **Hondo Crouch** in the 1970s. The

Luckenbach residents are proud of their modern communication facilities.

Many area motorcyclists meet in Luckenbach on Sunday afternoons to swap lies, kick tires, and drink Lone Star beer.

late Crouch used to invite his friends to stop by to play music, toss horse-shoes and washers, tell jokes and stories and just generally have a good ol' time. The rest of the world learned of Luckenbach when Willie Nelson and Waylon Jennings sang, " . . . in Luckenbach, Texas, ain't nobody feeling no pain . . ." and the town has become a mecca for country music fans.

The **Luckenbach General Store** also serves as a post office, souvenir shop, and bar. On weekends, shady picnic tables in back of the store provide a great setting for drinking Lone Star beer from long neck bottles, swapping lies, and listening to amateur guitar pickers plying their hobby. The old dance hall occasionally hosts name entertainers. It's a favorite Sunday after-noon destination for hundreds of bikers. Saturday is good too, but Sunday seems to be the big day. Should you visit Luckenbach on a Wednesday, you will find the whole town closed.

The ten acres that make up Luckenbach can even be rented for private events! Among the more infamous are the **Hell Hath No Fury Ladies State Chili Championship** (first Sat. in October), Texas' Independence Celebra-tion (March), and **Luckenbach's 4th of July Picnic** (sometimes hosted by Willie Nelson). For more info, surf over to www.luckenbachtexas.com.

After visiting Luckenbach, return to Hwy. 1376, turn left. Five miles will take you to the intersection with Hwy. 290. You are now only one left turn and 9 miles from completing your day as you return to Fredericksburg.

➡ Willie Nelson

If any one person can be credited with the popularity and evolution of country music since the 1970s, it would be Willie Nelson. Born in Abbott, Texas, on April 30, 1933, Nelson displayed his musical talent early in life, making his first musical performance at the age of 10 years, playing with a polka band. In 1961 he moved to Nashville, Tennessee, to start a career in country music. Although he was successful in writing several songs that became huge hits and country standards, they were originally recorded by other, better-known singers. The industry discouraged Nelson from becoming a singer himself, on the belief that his voice was not good enough nor his style traditional enough to be successful.

In 1970, Willie returned to his native Texas and began recording in Austin. The public flocked to the new sound and a string of number one hits soon followed. Nelson's appearance on stage, the content of his songs and his decision to record in Austin instead of Nashville soon branded him an "outlaw." Other performers followed suit, however, and Austin has grown into a major recording city for all types of music. Today, with more than 200 records selling over a million copies each, Willie Nelson has proven his talent beyond all doubts. He was inducted into the Country Music Hall of Fame in 1993, and has even starred in several hit movies.

But life has not always been good to Willie Nelson. He has suffered from bad marketing, and his troubles with the IRS are well known. His reputation as an avid pot smoker was confirmed when he was convicted for possession of cannabis. And, he has experienced many highly publicized personal problems along the way. These difficulties only made his fans love him more.

Today, making his home in the Texas Hill Country, Willie Nelson continues to perform around the world. He is the founder and primary force behind Farm Aid, and even has become a major spokesman for the Texas Department of Tourism, appearing in their commercials and inviting people "to come on down and visit Texas."   ✪

Day 12   Fredericksburg to New Braunsfels (SE Loop)

Distance *238 miles*

Features *This ride has more high-speed roads than the other loops. Couple that with a truly unique biker hangout in Canyon City, the always-popular River Road ride, and a visit to the oldest Dance Hall in Texas, and you have a lot in store. If you still haven't had enough, you can visit the larger Hill Country towns of New Bruanfels and San Marcos.*

From the intersection of Hwys. 290 and 16 in downtown Fredericksburg, take Hwy. 290 east for 6 miles, and turn right on Hwy. 1376. The twenty-eight mile ride to the intersection with Hwy. 87 just outside Boerne is, again, a typical Hill Country road that can be ridden at good speed. Turn left onto Hwy. 87 and in a mile and a half you will be at the Boerne town square. Turn left at the Exxon station onto Hwy. 474.

Boerne is another Hill Country town founded by German immigrants in the 1840s. Today, it has become quite an **artists' colony** and abounds with galleries and antique stores. A town of approximately 7,000 people, Boerne has more than 140 buildings dating back to its founding days. There seems

The oldest continuous German music band in the United States continues to perform on warm summer evenings in Boerne, Texas, and around the world.

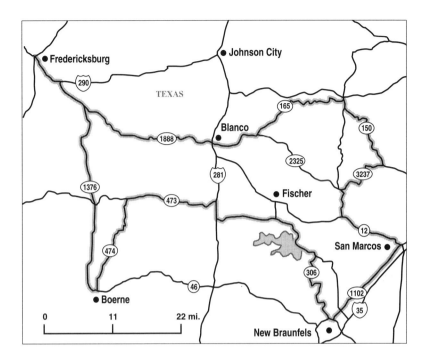

to be a festival of some sort nearly every weekend. The **Boerne Village Band,** the oldest German band in the U.S., travels all over the world performing Teutonic music specialties. On summer evenings, they a hold a concert series known as the *Abendkonzerte* in the town's main plaza.

After 18 miles, Hwy. 474 intersects with Hwy. 473; turn right and go 14 miles to the intersection with Hwy. 281. This 32-mile ride on Hwys. 474 and 473 are fairly typical Hill Country roads that can be ridden at fairly high speeds. Towards the end of this section, a few well-marked, sharp curves will require you to slow down.

Turn right onto Hwy. 281, go 3 miles, and then turn left onto Hwy. 306. After 18 miles of delightful riding, turn right onto Hwy. 2673 in Canyon City. If you look to your left at this intersection, you will see **The Shanty,** with, as the sign says, "Drinking and Dancing." It's a popular destination for weekend motorcyclists looking to take long neck beers out back and sit along the banks of the river on the shady grass. If it happens to be open when you go by, stop in and peruse the collection of bras dangling from the rafters. The skid marks on the dance floor were made by bikers who decided to "cut the rug" with their machines instead of their feet!

After only 2 miles on Hwy. 2673, turn left at the traffic signal in Sattler onto **River Road.** This road has earned its designation as one of the most

➡ Wildflowers

The roadsides and pasturelands of Texas are blanketed with blue, yellow, rust, and red wildflowers. Spring months in the hill country are worthy of a special note. Colorful autumn leaves lure others from different parts of the country. Monet would go wild! Just south of Austin, the National Wildflower Research Center (512-292-4200), founded by Lady Bird Johnson in 1982, contains interactive exhibits and examples of all the native fauna of Texas. To plan your trip for "peak" viewing, contact the state tourism bureau at 800-452-9292. As a rider, realize that at any time, you could round a turn on a small rural road only to find it all but blocked with cars and photographers.   ✪

If you ride the hill country in the spring, mile after mile of beautiful wildflowers will greet you.

The sign at this popular motorcycle stop leaves little doubt as to its purpose.

famous in the hill country, as it follows the **Guadalupe River** overhung with towering trees and stone cliffs. The speed limit is only 20 mph and you are well advised to obey it. Eleven miles later, at the T-intersection with River Road, turn left, proceed two more miles, and take a left turn onto Loop 337 just outside New Braunsfels.

✪ Side Trip

The first exit off Loop 337 offers you the opportunity to visit the historic town of **Gruene**. It has been carefully restored and contains the oldest dance hall in Texas, where country greats, such as **George Strait, Bo Diddley, The Dixie Chicks, Jerry Lee Lewis, Garth Brooks,** and **Willie Nelson,** have performed. The hall was also used as a set in the movie *Michael,* starring **John Travolta.** Upon exiting, turn left.

After your visit, return and continue down Loop 337 until you intersect with I-35 Business. At this intersection, turn left. If you wish to visit downtown New Braunsfels, turn right here.

New Braunsfels sits at the intersection of the Comal and Guadalupe Rivers. With a population approaching 35,000, it is the second largest city in the Hill Country. Just another one of the many towns and cities that have

You'll find action any night in Gruene at the oldest dance hall in Texas.

grown from the German settlements of the 1840s, today New Braunsfels honors these roots with good German food and architecture. The annual **Wurstfest** in November features local sausages and German bands in traditional garb. Of special interest to the biker is the **Alamo Classic Car Museum** located on I-35 between Exits 180 and 182. The huge facility houses more than 150 restored antique automobiles, motorcycles, and fire trucks. If you have time to eat, try **Krause's Café** at 148 S. Castell for some local German favorites.

I-35 Business runs beside the actual interstate for a mile or two before intersecting with Hwy. 306, where you need to make a left turn. In addition to the **New Braunsfels Visitors' Center,** you will find a couple of **motorcycle dealerships** along this short stretch, should you need to have your bike serviced.

After 1 mile on Hwy. 306, turn right onto Hwy. 1102, for a fairly straight, flat seven miles to the intersection with Hwy. 2439; go straight ahead onto Hwy. 2439. After 11 miles, turn left onto Hwy. 12.

✪ *Side Trip*

If you want to visit downtown **San Marcos,** just go straight ahead at the previous intersection. In a few short blocks you will be in the town square. San Marcos, with a population approaching 40,000, is

➡ Texas Wine

Franciscan padres planted the first grapevines in Texas in 1662, nearly a century before cultivation started in California. The weather and soil conditions in certain parts of the state are almost perfect for growing grapes and, until Prohibition, Texas led the nation in wine production. Today, Texas ranks fifth among wine producing states, and it markets many of its wares to France. The Hill Country alone has more than 16 wineries where you are welcome to drop in for free tours and daily tastings.

Most Texas wines are varietals; that is, they are made almost entirely from the type of grape listed on the bottle. The cabernet sauvignon, merlot, chardonnay, and pinot noir are considered the best and are the most popular. These fine wines are often proudly referred to as "Chateau de Bubba" and "Vin de Lone Star." For more information, call the Texas Department of Agriculture (512-463-7624) and request their free brochure, *Texas Wine Country Tour Guide.* ★

located on the eastern edge of the Hill Country on the **San Marcos River.** Although it was named by the Spanish, who found it on St. Marks Day, they were never successful in establishing themselves here. It was up to the European immigrants that arrived in the 1846 to found the town.

Relaxing by your tent after a good day's ride is what motorcycle touring is all about.

San Marcos has an interesting town center and has two areas that are **National Register Historic Places:** the downtown district, and the San Antonio and Belvin Streets residential districts. There is a two-mile long scenic walkway along the river that starts just two blocks from the courthouse on the town square. It is famous locally for the huge outlet malls on the outskirts of town along I-35.

After 10 miles Hwy. 12 goes to the right; take this turn and continue on Hwy. 12 for 5 more miles. Take a right turn onto Hwy. 3237 in Wimberley. If you are hungry, **Wimberley** has several places for a meal or snack. Just past the intersection of Hwys. 12 and 3237, there's a good Bar-B-Q place on the right that offers outdoor dining.

Soon, you will be leaving the built-up area around New Braunsfels and San Marcos to get back to some wonderful Hill Country riding. After 12 miles, turn left onto Hwy. 150 west in Hays City (one general store); this is an easy turn to miss, so be on the look out. After 11 delightful miles of riding, take a right turn onto Hwy. 12; two miles later, go left onto Hwy. 290 in Dripping Springs. Go less than a mile down Hwy. 290 and take a left onto Hwy. 190 (Creek Road). The sign is very small, but there is a larger sign indicating Loop 64 opposite it.

Many street names in the small towns of the Hill Country retain their original German names.

Creek Road becomes a one-lane, two-way road—one of many that exist in the Hill Country. It also has several one-lane bridges along its 9-mile path. This is just another (ho-hum) super bike ride. Three miles after the turn-off from Hwy. 290, Creek Road intersects with County Road 220 and makes a right turn (don't go straight on County Road 220). At the intersection with Hwy. 165, take a left.

Hwy. 165 runs alongside the **Blanco River.** After 15 miles, at the T-intersection with Loop 163, take a right into Blanco. When Loop 163 intersects with Hwy. 281, go straight across, to get on Hwy. 1623. After 5 miles, turn left onto Hwy. 1888. The 28 miles to the intersection with Hwy. 1376 are just great, high-speed, Hill Country roads.

Turn right onto Hwy. 1376. If you haven't yet visited **Luckenbach,** go 2 miles up Hwy. 1376 and turn left just across the bridge. After seven miles on Hwy. 1376, turn left onto Hwy. 290. Five miles later, you will be in Fredericksburg.

Day 13   Fredericksburg to Y.O. Ranch (W Loop)

Distance *215 miles*

Features *This loop consists mostly of high-speed roads that are somewhat straighter than usual for the Hill Country. However, you will find many curves, sweepers, and twisties along the way. While it is set up as a one-day trip, I recommend you make it a two-day ride with an overnight stop at the Y.O. Ranch. In spite of the deserted countryside, there are plenty of small towns to visit along the way.*

From the intersection of Hwys. 290/87 and 16 in Fredericksburg, take Hwy. 16 south for approximately four miles and then make a right turn onto Hwy. 2093. The 22 miles that follow are a lot flatter and straighter than most Hill Country roads, but you are treated to an almost constant view of the beautiful terrain through which you are riding.

Turn left onto Hwy. 290 in Harper, go four miles, and then turn right onto Hwy. 479. The constant up and down and up and down on this road will remind you of a roller coaster thickly lined with cedar trees. In the Hill Country, **cedar trees** are considered a nuisance, as they tend to choke out the live oak trees. It is unusual to see such an abundant growth, as most landowners clear them out.

After about 20 miles, at a T-intersection, turn right onto Hwy. 2169, toward the town of Junction. Four miles later, as you are approaching the intersection with I-10, turn right just before the STOP sign to continue on Hwy. 2169. Along this stretch, notice the many pecan groves with huge trees. The pecans that have been developing here since 1896 are known throughout the world. The **Oliver pecan,** named after the man who developed them, can produce up to 350 to 400 pounds of nuts per year.

After approximately 9 miles you will be approaching I-10. Take the overpass across the interstate, proceed one mile, then turn right onto Loop 481. You will enter the town of Junction upon crossing the river.

About one mile after turning onto Loop 481, take a left onto Hwy. 377. Prepare for 43 miles of magnificent motorcycling. Four miles along this wonderful road, you will find the **South Llano River State Park,** an excellent public park with camping facilities, hiking trails, river tubing, and many other activities. The deer, wild turkeys, and wildlife for which the park is known are somewhat accustomed to people and can be viewed at very close range. If you are a camper, an overnight stay here would be a true joy. If you

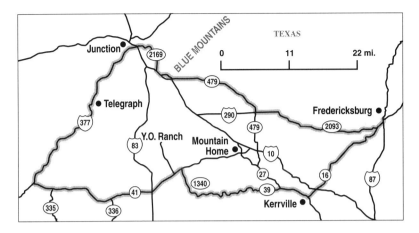

just want to ride through and see the wildlife, let them know at the entrance and the $3 entrance fee will be waived for your short visit.

While Hwy. 377 is a major thruway, it is considered by many to be the most scenic road in the Hill Country. From the motorcyclist's viewpoint, it is not only scenic, but also a great ride. While you can make good time on this road, it does have a few surprises; I suggest you keep your speed down; many of the curves along this ride have a suggested 30 mph speed limit. Enjoy the high limestone cliffs along the **South Llano River** covered with trees and other vegetation.

After 43 miles of fun on Hwy. 377, turn left onto Hwy. 41, which is more high-speed than Hwy. 377. After about 33 miles, the entrance to the Y.O. Ranch will be on your left. Once consisting of more than 500,000 acres, the **Y.O. Ranch** is now only a measly (by Texas standards) 40,000 acres. But to put that in perspective: it is more than seven miles from the entrance gate to the lodge. I highly recommend a visit. A handy café, the **Chuckwagon,** serves three meals a day that are included in the price of your room.

More than 10,000 animals roam freely over the Y.O. Ranch, more than 60 percent of which are exotics from all over the world (mostly Africa). A hunter can choose his prey from upwards of forty species, which include addax ($5,000), dama gazelle ($4,500) or, for those of you on a budget, wild turkey (only $450). Of course, these fees do not include the $200 fee and a tip for your guide, who can also provide you with a rifle and other equipment. Hone your skills before embarking, as a wounded animal costs just as much as a kill here.

Many people come to the Y.O. Ranch to hunt with only a camera. A two-hour tour ($30 including a meal) is available several times a day. The giraffe will eat corn from your hand. Bring plenty of film and enjoy your safari! A one-day advance reservation is required for tours and lodging.

Although exotic animals are the big draw, the Y.O. remains a working cattle ranch, and the friendly staff can help you schedule some horseback riding. If you time it right, you could even go on an overnight cattle drive (a la *City Slickers*).

In spite of the size of this place, there are limited camping and motel accommodations, so plan your visit for during the week and give as much advance notice as possible (800-967-2624; www.yoranch.com). Rooms run about $80 per person, per night, and include three meals and a free open bar in the evening for several hours. There is a very nice swimming pool and hot tub near the lodging area. RV camping costs $20 per night.

After your visit to the ranch, return to the main road, continue east on Hwy. 41 for another two miles, and then turn right onto Hwy. 1340, a road for which Hill Country riding is famous. It has something for everyone: sport bikers can test themselves and their machines and cruisers can enjoy the wonderful scenery.

After about 19 miles, you will encounter another of those almost endless oddities that cover Texas and reflect the eclectic natures of its residents. On the right side of the road, sitting in a pasture, is a **full-size model of**

Texans love exotic animal ranches. You never know what you'll see around the next bend. (photo by Jack Lewis/TxDOT)

At the Y.O. Ranch, a hunter with about $5,000 handy could take aim at this fellow. Many folks come to take a tour and merely photo-hunt.

Stonehenge, in better repair than the original in England. You are welcomed to visit the site at no charge.

Twenty-one miles after turning on Hwy. 1340, turn left onto Hwy. 39 toward Ingram. Rolling along the **Guadalupe River,** this road begs to be enjoyed. While fairly well developed, there is usually little or no traffic along it during the week. After only six miles, you will come to the intersection with Hwy. 27, where the road becomes four-lane as it approaches Kerrville (see Day 11). Seven miles after passing through Kerrville, turn left onto Hwy. 16. Fredericksburg is only 25 miles up the road.

Day 14   Fredericksburg to San Antonio

Distance *90 miles*

Features *Visit a wildflower farm—an opportunity you don't want to miss in the spring; take a short side trip to the LBJ Ranch complex if you didn't have the time on Day 9. You'll end up near the San Antonio airport.*

From downtown Fredericksburg, proceed east on Hwy. 290. About 8 miles later, start looking for the wildflower ranch on your left—a clearly marked, multi-story building sitting out in the middle of a field. In the spring and summer, with the wildflowers blooming, it is an incredible feast for the eyes.

After 16 miles on this good, high speed, four-lane road, turn right onto Hwy. 1623. The **LBJ Ranch** complex is only two miles down Hwy. 290 from this turn, should you wish to visit (see Day 9).

Hwy. 1623 twists and turns, and goes up and down, often running alongside the **Blanco River.** After 16 miles of this fun, turn right onto County Road 103, which has a posted speed limit of 30 mph. It has a few river crossings that could be wet after a rainy spell, as well as some open range sections. Slow down and enjoy!

At the T-intersection, take a left. Some 6 miles after turning onto Trainer West, take the right turn at the T-intersection onto Ficher Street. You will be in Blanco, a few short blocks from where you will turn right onto Hwy. 281. Eight miles later, turn right onto Hwy. 473. After 8 miles on Hwy. 473, make a left turn onto Hwy. 3351 in Kendalia.

Savor the remaining 23 miles to I-10, before you start to see more development, with huge ranch houses sitting atop the hills alongside the road. Take I-10 east and 13 miles later you will be at the intersection with Loop 410. To get to the airport area, take Loop 410 east.

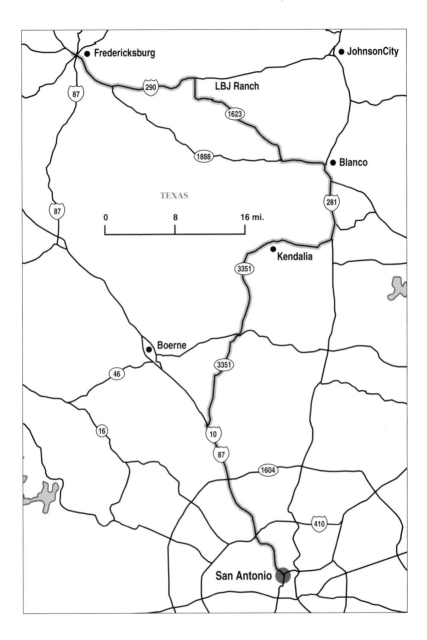

Day 15   Day Loop From San Antonio

Distance *350 miles*

Features *If your time is limited, this loop is an excellent introduction to Hill Country riding—you just might find yourself planning to return for a longer visit. Don't let today's distance discourage you: the first 90 miles consist of good high-speed roads in the 70–80 mph range. Two of the roads included in this loop, Hwys. 335 and 337, are considered by many to be the crème de la crème of Hill Country riding.*

Starting at the intersection of Loop 410 and Hwy. 90 on the western side of San Antonio, head west on Hwy. 90 for approximately 73 miles before turning right onto Hwy. 55 in Uvalde.

Uvalde is a fairly typical small central Texas town with a population numbering under 5,000, and a fierce pride in its past. **Pat Garrett** moved to Uvalde after killing Billy the Kid. It is the hometown of **Dale Evans** and was the home of **John "Cactus Jack" Nance Garner,** one of many famous Texas politicians who was vice president of the U.S. during Franklin Roosevelt's first two terms. His nickname derived from his efforts to have the cactus as Texas' state flower (it lost to the bluebonnet by one vote). Today,

During your rides in the hill country, you will experience many ups and downs with blind curves.

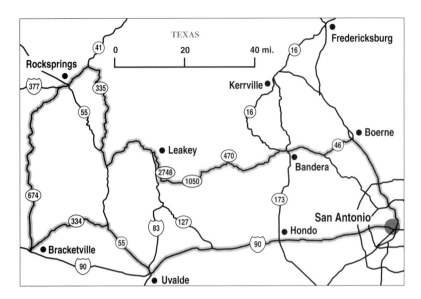

Uvalde makes for a nice stop, with quiet streets, antique shops, boutiques, and other tourist traps. For a trip into the past, try the **Rexall Drug and Soda Fountain** located at 201 N. Getty Street, the oldest retail establishment in the city, in operation since 1883.

After only two miles, Hwy. 55 splits with Hwy. 83; turn left and continue on Hwy. 55. It's a fairly straight, flat road, but one with first-rate views of the upcoming Hill Country ride off to your right. After approximately 18 miles, turn left onto Hwy. 334, which is narrow with no shoulders. There is often tall grass and brush growing right up to, and sometimes onto, the road-way. I suggest you slow down and keep a sharp eye out for wildlife. After 29 miles of riding through these gentle curves and modest hills, turn right at the T-intersection onto Hwy. 674, just north of Brackettville.

About seven miles up Hwy. 674, you'll find the **Alamo Village** (www.alamovillage.com) off to your right, a Hollywood stage set that has been used in more than a hundred major movies, TV shows, documentaries, commercials, and music videos. It all began in 1957, with the construction of a historically correct replica of the 1836 Alamo, and was used in the filming of *The Alamo,* starring **John Wayne.** Other films have included *Texas Rangers, A Certain Kind of Man* and the **Willie Nelson** music video *Tougher than Leather.*

Follow Hwy. 674 for about 56 miles and turn right onto Hwy. 377 toward Rocksprings. After a fairly straight and flat start through open scrubland covered with cactus, yucca, and mesquite, the road starts its climb into the Hill Country—curving and twisting along the side of hills with rivers and valleys below. Tie up your leathers and put a grin on your face, because it only gets better as the day goes on!

Proceed on Hwy. 377 through the city of **Rocksprings.** There are several turns, but all are clearly marked. For eight miles out of Rocksprings, enjoy the wonderful sweepers before turning right onto Hwy. 41. Four miles later, turn right onto Hwy. 335, one of the most famous and best-loved rides in the Hill Country. The sign says it all: BEWARE - STEEP GRADES AND SHARP CURVES. This next 29 miles is some serious motorcycling. You can test your skills or just slow down and enjoy the wonderful vistas as you squirrel your way along cliffs and cuts through the rugged terrain. Note: there are several spots on the road strewn with rocks and pebbles from the cliffs above.

Turn left onto Hwy. 55, go about 5 miles, and then hook a left onto Hwy. 337 toward Leakey. To know what to expect for the next 21 miles, just re-read the previous paragraph. This is another "ho-hum" Hill Country route. Be sure to take a double dose of your heart medication before setting out.

Turn left onto Hwy. 1120 just south of Leakey, continue for seven miles, and turn left onto Hwy. 2748, which is a nice, meandering motorcycle road with creek crossings and easy curves. After only two miles, turn left onto Hwy. 1050, follow this excellent motorcycle road for about 13 miles, and take a left onto Hwy. 187. Hwy. 1050 is wonderful, but not as dramatic as the previous highways.

After three miles on Hwy. 187, take a right onto Hwy. 470. This is a good ride with occasional sections that can be ridden at pretty good speed—but don't let this lure you into non-alertness. Most of this road has sharp curves that will bite the casual or non-attentive rider! There is also unusually heavy vegetation along the sides of the roads, and these trees and bushes provide a great hiding place for animals. Beware!

After approximately 28 miles, turn right at the T-intersection onto Hwy. 16—a major highway, but a pleasant ride nonetheless. Follow the signs through the small town of Bandera. Approximately 14 miles after joining Hwy. 16, turn left onto Hwy. 46 toward Boerne. After about 11 miles of super-nice Hill Country riding, get on I-10 east, and you will be only 25 miles to the intersection with Loop 410 on the northwest outskirts of San Antonio.

✪ *Options*

For the best riding between Fredericksburg and Rocksprings, use the route on Day 12 until you get to Leakey, then continue on Hwy. 337 to Camp Wood, where you pick up Hwy. 55 to Rocksprings. If you're going from Rocksprings to Fredericksburg, head south on Hwy. 55, and in Camp Wood, turn left onto Hwy. 337. When you arrive in Leakey, pick up directions to Fredericksburg as outlined on Day 12.

Should you wish a more direct route from Fredericksberg to Rocksprings, take Hwy. 16 south for 24 miles, turn west on I-10, and go 16 miles to the Mountain Home Exit, where you will pick up Hwy. 41 west. Fifty one miles later, at the T-intersection, turn left onto Hwy. 377, and you'll be only 8 miles from Rocksprings. Reverse these directions if you are traveling from Rocksprings to Fredericksburg. This 100-mile ride should take no more than three hours and will give you the opportunity to familiarize yourself with your new home base.

Day 16   San Antonio to Rocksprings

Distance *150 miles*

Features *For the next few days you will be getting away from tourist stops and into rural "down-home" Texas to experience the joys of Hill Country riding!*

From the intersection of I-10 and Loop 410 on the northwest side of San Antonio (near the airport), take 410 west for approximately 11 miles and then take the Culbera Road Exit to get onto Hwy. 3487. You will be on a frontage road for a short mile or so before taking a right onto the actual highway at the first traffic signal. A block later, turn left onto Hwy. 1957.

After the intersection with Loop 1604, Hwy. 1957 becomes a two-laner and you will have left the city. Eight miles after leaving the interstate, turn right onto Hwy. 471 at the T-intersection, follow Hwy. 471 for 10 miles, then take a left onto Hwy. 1283. Highway 471 runs through flat farming land, but for some reason, it contains several 90-degree turns—not all of which are marked. Since you can see all the way through these turns, however, they can be taken safely at fairly high speeds.

Turn left at the T-intersection onto Hwy. 16 in Pipe Creek and follow this road for 22 miles to the intersection of Hwy. 337 in Medina, **one of the premier routes in the Hill Country,** and one which will become an old friend

Views like this give you one more reason to ride slowly.

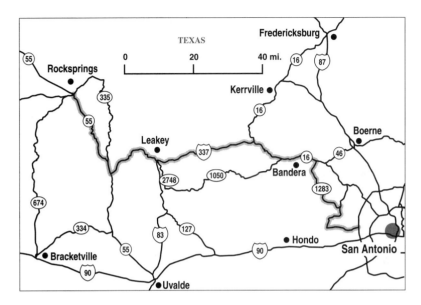

and favorite of yours also. Parts of Hwy. 337 are included in at least two of the loops you will be riding. Continue on Hwy. 337 for about 50 miles then turn right onto Hwy. 55 in Camp Wood where you should turn right. From that point, it will be only 38 miles of good, scenic, high-speed, two-lane highway until you arrive in Rocksprings.

Rocksprings (pop.1,700) sits at an altitude of 2,400 ft. (high by Hill Country standards). Located at the intersection of Hwys. 55 and 377 on the western edge of the **Edwards Plateau** which forms the Hill Country, don't expect to find many establishments catering to the tourist trade in Rocksprings. Do your strolling and shopping elsewhere; come here to sit back, listen to the locals discuss weather and politics, and enjoy a meal in a local café. There are no "restaurants" in Rocksprings, but you won't starve in this town if you hanker for fine home cooking followed by homemade pie.

The eponymous spring that seemed to flow directly from a rock on the north side of town is long dry. These days, the main industry around here is sheep farming. In 1926, angora goat breeders established their headquarters in Rocksprings, and the town duly became known as the **Angora Goat Capitol of the World.** Angora goats produce a long, silky wool called mohair, and for many years, the federal government subsidized this industry since mohair was important in the manufacturing of military uniforms. With the advent of new materials, more and more garments stopped using mohair, and the subsidies gradually faded, leaving the industry a shadow of its former self.

If like staying in historic hotels, try the Rocksprings Hotel in "downtown" Rocksprings.

While a mohair warehouse serves as a central shipping point for this material, the only retail outlet that carries products made from "the diamond fabric" is **Mohair Fashions and Gifts,** located on Main Street. A visit to the Angora Goat Breeders Museum on Austin Street will give you a good picture of the mohair industry in its heyday. The second largest contributor to the Rocksprings economy is hunting. The local paper is filled with ads for hunting trips, guide services, taxidermy, etc.

Lodging choices are slim in Rocksprings: the **Rocksprings Hotel** ($60; 830-683-4242), located on the town square at 200 W. Austin, is somewhat overpriced in my opinion, but it does have a wonderful history. Established in 1916 as the Gilmore Hotel, the place originally served traveling salesmen, local ranchers, and other visitors. At one time, its kitchen was well thought-of, and even served food to the prisoners in the jail across the street. Over the years, the Rocksprings Hotel has sheltered influenza patients and victims of a 1927 tornado. About half the rooms are furnished with period furniture, but with all the modern amenities; the other half are under renovation.

An alternative lodging is the **Mesa Motel** ($35; 830-683-3241) at 105 E. Main Street, a clean and adequate joint, well-known among the area's hunters. The closest campground to Rocksprings is located just south of the intersection of Hwys. 55 and 337 in Camp Wood (830-597-3223), with scenic and relaxing sites along the **Nuecus River** ($10 per night for two; $5 each additional camper). Or, try the **Big Oak River Camp** located about five miles south of Camp Wood on Hwy. 55 (830-597-5280; their web site is www.bigoakrivercamp.com). Tent camping on this 51-acre site will cost about $15 per night. It is located in a beautiful pecan grove and has all the necessities, including showers, toilets, and laundry.

While your dining options are limited in Rocksprings, you do have a few options. Try **Vaquero's Ranchhouse,** located on Hwy. 377 just north of town (830-683-4369). This establishment not only offers passable Tex-Mex food, it also has a full-service menu. **Ben & Company** (830-683-4470), the local Shell and Texaco station, serves up a variety of home-cooked specials, which include everything from breakfast burritos to chicken gizzards and egg rolls. There are also several typical fast food joints located around town.

Nightlife is sparse in Rocksprings. However, **Devil's Sinkhole State Natural Area** is one natural attraction worth a visit. Located on private property about six miles north of Rocksprings, you can only access the site at certain times, during a guided tour. The sinkhole opens into a vast underground cavern that is the home for **millions of Brazilian freetail bats** from early May until late October. At dusk, the sight of all these bats exiting the cavern for a night of hunting is not to be missed. For information, contact the **Devil's Sinkhole Society** (830-683-2287; www.tpwd.state.tx.us/park/sinkhole/sinkhole.htm.) All tours leave from a visitors' center located at 101 N. Sweeten Street in downtown Rocksprings.

Day 17   Rocksprings to Caverns (NW Loop)

Distance *250 miles*

Features *This loop will take you onto the Great Plains, for a different view of Texas. Visit what experts have called, "the most beautiful cave in the world," as well as a restored Old West fort. The day ends with some memorable riding.*

From the square in downtown Rocksprings, take Hwy. 55 north for approximately 33 miles, then turn right onto Hwy. 277 toward Sonora. The previous section is not great motorcycling, but the countryside can be fun. As you leave Rocksprings, you will realize that you are leaving the Hill Country. As you lose altitude, the hills become farther apart and the dry, less vegetated, terrain becomes covered with boulders.

Many of the "rivers" in the Hill Country are dry most of the time. However, they can become raging torrents after heavy rains. Be on the lookout for flooding during these periods.

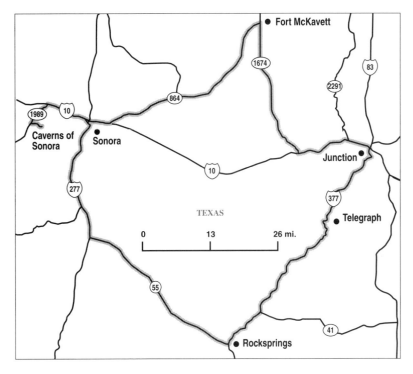

After approximately 20 miles on Hwy. 277, you will be approaching the town of Sonora. The **Great Plains** stretch out ahead. Don't fear, you will be back in the Hill Country soon. Take a right at the bypass sign indicating I-10 west and continue on for about 8 miles. Take Exit 39 and turn left under the interstate onto Hwy. 1989. Six miles later, turn left into the Caverns of Sonora, located about one mile down this narrow paved road.

○ *Side Trip*

The **Caverns of Sonora** are unique in that they contain many crystal formations, including some that grow sideways instead of vertically. A past president of the National Speleological Society said, "This is the most indescribably beautiful cavern in the world. Its beauty cannot be exaggerated, even by Texans!" Daily tours are ranked from "easy" (lasting about an hour) to "rigorous" (which can last up to 4 ½ hours and include crawling through narrow spaces and using ropes to access certain areas). If you are not physically fit, the operators recommend you skip the longer tours. Call ahead for reservations or information (915-387-3105; www.cavernsofsonora.com).

Fort McKavett is wonderfully restored, has a rich history, and the walking tour is worth the stop.

After you visit to the caverns, retrace your route to I-10, go east 10 miles, and take Exit 404 onto Hwy. 864, on which you will head northeast toward Fort McKavett. After approximately 37 miles of fairly straightforward, high-speed road, you will reach the intersection with Hwy. 1674. A half-mile later on Hwy. 864 you will see Fort McKavett.

Today, **Fort McKavett** (915-396-2358) sits among oak trees in an idyllic setting along the **San Saba River.** One can only imagine how remote and tranquil this location must have been at the time of its establishment in 1852. Built of locally available limestone, oak, and pecan wood, the fort was founded to protect travelers on the El Paso Road (primarily heading for the California gold fields) from the Apache and Comanche Indians. It was abandoned in 1859 as the Indian threat diminished, and it remained that way until after the Civil War.

During the Civil War, Indians retook lands in the area and Fort McKavett was reopened at the conclusion of hostilities. At its peak, it housed up to 400 troops and civilians, including many of the famous "buffalo soldiers." It was re-abandoned in 1883, when the Indians were once again deemed no longer a threat, and local settlers moved into the existing buildings, which accounts for why the site is so well preserved today. Many structures have been restored to their original condition. Named a **Texas State Historic Site** in 1968, the displays include interpretive exhibits, period photos, and hundreds of artifacts. Plan your day to spend and hour or so on the well laid-out walking tour.

After your visit to the fort, return to Hwy. 1674, turn left, and head south for approximately 28 miles to the intersection of I-10. Initially this ride is straight, but the road is narrow and lacks shoulders, with vegetation coming right up to the roadway. The abundance of wildlife in the area has caused the State of Texas to lower the speed limit to 60 mph. Stay alert at all times.

It will soon be obvious that you are re-entering the Hill Country proper, as the hills and curves become more frequent. Go under I-10 and continue on Hwy. 1674, for approximately 10 miles, into the town of Junction (I-10 will be on your left and in sight for most of this ride). Turn right onto Hwy. 377 south in Junction, and proceed 49 miles to return to Rocksprings (watch for the turn at the first light in town; follow signs for Hwy. 377). Most maps indicate this ride to be scenic; these maps are correct. While it's a somewhat faster ride than most Hill Country roads, the twists and turns will keep you very happy.

Day 18   Rocksprings to Camp Wood (SE Loop)

Distance *170 miles*

Features *You'll have a full day of riding on magnificent roads. A visit to beautiful Gardner State Park, a quaint lunch stop steeped in history, and a secluded artists' colony round out the day.*

Leave Rocksprings via Hwy. 377 heading north. After 8 miles, turn right onto Hwy. 41, and a mile later you will spot a picnic area on the left that has a dramatic overlook of the Hill Country. Approximately 5 miles after getting on Hwy. 41, turn right onto Hwy. 335. This "typical" Hill Country route offers 27 miles of delightful riding. Note that this very narrow, two-lane road

Frequent rockslides can create quite a hazard for a rider. You should stay vigilant when entering a blind curve, as a surprise may wait ahead.

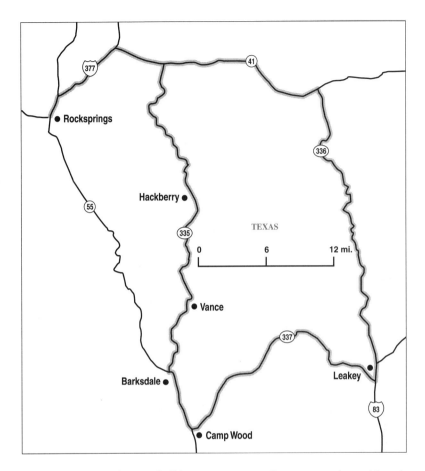

requires extra caution; rockslides are common. On most sections, 45 mph will be your posted speed limit. Turn left onto Hwy. 55 in Barksdale and five miles later you will be in Camp Wood.

Camp Wood advertises itself as "conveniently located in the middle of nowhere." That's about right. In Camp Wood, turn left onto Hwy. 337, the road *Ride Texas* magazine describes as the **Best Motorcycle Road in Texas.** After 21 miles of as-good-as-it-gets you will arrive in Leakey. Unless you are a big-time road racer, it will take you about 45 minutes to cover this stretch. In Leakey, turn right onto Hwy. 83 south, a major two-lane highway along the Frio River, which, nevertheless, makes for a lovely ride. After 9 miles, turn left onto Park Road 29 to enter **Gardner State Park,** the most visited state park in Texas. Camping and shelters are available.

Return to Hwy. 83, turn left, proceed 7 miles, then turn left onto Hwy. 127 toward the town of Concan (pop. 71).

On weekends, local bikers fill the Hill Country to ride the great roads and gather at roadside eating places. Riding on weekdays will find the road almost deserted.

At the **Frio River** crossing, **Neal's Lodging** is an interesting place to visit and perhaps grab a burger. Built in 1929, this place still utilizes the original buildings, and it has a good restaurant with a rock patio and cedar wood tables. Inside, the walls are covered with photos dating back to the early days.

After your visit to Neal's, return to Hwy. 83 and turn left (south) toward Leakey. Three miles along, you will spot a sign for **Reagan Wells,** an artists' colony with potters, painters, and metal sculptors. This can make for an interesting side trip, but note that there is a good bit of dirt about five miles in, though it is usually in good shape and I believe would cause no problems for any competently ridden motorcycle.

Return to Hwy. 83, turn north, and return the 14 miles to Leakey. About a half-mile north of Leakey, turn left onto Hwy. 336, yet another "ho-hum" incredible Hill Country road. Twenty-eight delightful miles later, turn left onto Hwy. 41, proceed about 15 miles, and turn left onto Hwy. 377 at the T-intersection. In 9 miles you will re-enter Rocksprings.

Day 19   Rocksprings to Alamo Village (SW Loop)

Distance *180 miles*

Features *The riding is great and the roadside attractions are of the sort you'll only find in Texas.*

From downtown Rocksprings, take Hwy. 377 west for 5 miles or so, turn left onto Hwy. 674, and after 67 miles of suburb Hill Country riding you will see the **Alamo Village** on the left, a true must-stop worth at least a couple of hours. Originally built for the 1959 movie *Alamo,* starring **John Wayne,** the creators were aiming for an authentic reproduction of San Antonio in the early 1800s. At a cost of more than twelve million dollars, *Alamo* held the brief distinction of being the most expensive movie ever filmed.

Since then, Alamo Village (830-563-2580; www.alamovillage.com) has been used in more than 100 movies, alternately depicting a rural Mexican village, fort, frontier town, and hacienda. It is still in use today, and you could be lucky enough to catch some filming during your visit. The ranch which contains the set has a hotel, motel, and places to eat. If you've never seen a **Texas long-horned cow,** you'll get a chance here.

After your visit continue 7 miles south on Hwy. 674 to Brackettville, a fairly straight, high-speed run as the terrain flattens out.

◊ *Side Trip*

When you get to the intersection with Hwy. 90, take a right and then turn left at the first light. After about a mile, you'll see the **Seminole Indian Scout Cemetery.** In the early 1800s black slaves fled to Florida and joined the Seminole Indians, among whom they worked, lived, and intermarried. They fought against the U.S. Army during its campaign against the Seminole. After the Civil War, the U.S. Army recruited some as scouts to eliminate the Apache and Comanche.

Much of the population of Brackettville was black, Indian, or Hispanic, and today's population are their descendants. Four of those buried here earned the **Congressional Medal of Honor** for their service to our country (three during the Indian wars, and one during the war with Mexico). The site is well maintained.

Return to Hwy. 90 and take a right to Brackettville. **Fort Clark Spring** *is* Brackettville. The imposing stone entranceway is impossible to miss. Many of the original buildings are still in use today; the barracks is now a hotel. Of

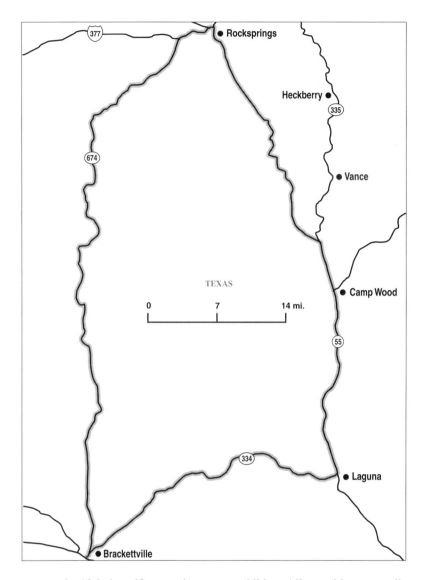

course, the 18-hole golf course is a newer addition. All amenities are available in the fort. If you have the time, this can be a wonderful overnight stop.

Exiting Fort Clark Spring, continue one half-mile on Hwy. 90 and then turn left onto Hwy. 334. The next 26 miles will take you back into the Hill Country on a good high-speed road. At the intersection, turn left onto Hwy. 55 north, a major two-laner that is nevertheless a beautiful 69-mile ride. The last half from Barksdale to Rocksprings is really nice—up-and-downs with plenty of twisties.

Day 20   Rocksprings to San Antonio

Distance *150 miles*

Features *This day gives you a last good chance to ride some familiar Hill Country terrain before gradually descending to the flatlands as you approach San Antonio and its ever-present traffic.*

From Rocksprings, take Hwy. 55 south for approximately 38 miles to Camp Wood. Turn left onto Hwy. 337 toward Medina, and enjoy the next 50 miles of this wonderful road, as it will be the final Hill Country road to remember when you look back on this trip.

Turn right onto Hwy. 16 in Medina, and for next 22 miles you'll gradually begin your descent. The Hill Country will be in your rear-view mirror. Turn right onto Hwy. 1283 in Pipe Creek. After 23 miles of gentle hills, turn right onto Hwy. 471, a flat stretch with farm and pastureland on either side. You can make good speed, but the road does have several unmarked 90-degree turns, though you can see all the way through them.

Always be alert for these guys (and gals) when riding Hill Country roads!

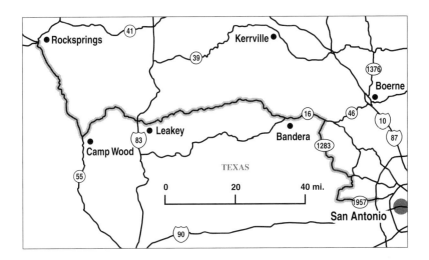

Turn left onto Hwy. 1957, which will become a four-laner as you pass under Loop 1604 and get immersed in the swarming traffic of San Antonio. At
the intersection of I-410, go east for 11 miles to the intersection with I-10.

Houston The Coastal Route

Starting and ending in Houston, this route consists of six days of riding and covers more than 1,200 miles of seacoast and marshland, brushy scrublands with rolling hills, and live oak forests. This area also showcases the diverse people who call themselves Texans; from the sophisticated of metropolitan Houston to the laid-back fishermen in the coastal regions. The rolling hills of mesquite and cactus in south central Texas to the border with Mexico, and the large Hispanic population there gives you a flavor of life in that nation.

Approaching a population of nearly two million, **Houston** is the fourth largest city in the United States. It is a sprawling metropolis containing more than 500 square miles within its city limits. Skyscrapers leap from the flat landscape like weeds in a well-groomed lawn—works of structural art in their own right. At night, these clusters of giants glow with light, creating a truly awesome sight. The terrain is flat and low with the highest elevation in the city limits reaching only ninety feet above sea level. Houston is the second largest international seaport in the country, although it is more than fifty

Skyscrapers sprout like mushrooms from the flat lands on which Houston is located. (photo by Jack Lewis/TxDOT)

*Riders do enjoy
the Texas
weather.*

miles from the Gulf of Mexico. As you would expect from a city this size, Houston has more than 200 museums, cultural sites, and other places to visit. Houstonians are very proud of their arts. Their symphony, ballet, and theater are comparable to any in the world.

Houston was founded by **John** and **Augustus Allen** in 1836, when they established a trading post on **Buffalo Bayou.** The climate was truly brutal with heat, high humidity, and insects. From the beginning, Houston established a reputation for being a rough-and-tumble, high-stakes city, and it works hard to maintain that reputation to this day. The Houston attitude is exemplified in the city's zoning laws: they have none.

Houston's location and climate kept its development moving at a slow pace until the 1930s; the miracle of air conditioning, however, changed all that. Today, most Houstonians move from their air-conditioned homes to their air-conditioned cars to their air-conditioned workplaces, rarely encountering the sweltering heat. Some of the parking lots in Houston are even air conditioned. A new visitor often notes that there is almost no pedestrian traffic downtown, even during a lunch hour on a working day. In fact, there is a huge underground tunnel system (air-conditioned, of course) that connects most of the downtown buildings, and contains shops, restaurants, and everything else one should need in daily life.

With the discovery of massive amounts of oil at **Spindletop** in 1901, Houston quickly became the new hub for the oil business. Today it is estimated that 35 percent of its economy is based on oil and oil related businesses. All major companies and hundreds of independents are represented, and some of them claim Houston as their home. The influx of money they bring to the city is a boon for local entrepreneurs who are interested in serving their needs. As a result, the shopping opportunities are limitless.

Although the oil industry brings in the money, the **Texas Medical Center** is the largest employer in Houston. Consisting of more than 40 institutions covering almost 700 acres near downtown, they offer state-of-the-art medical services to a worldwide clientele. For more information on things to see and do in Houston check out their visitors' center website at www.houston-guide.com.

Houston has two major airports, **George Bush Intercontinental,** located 20 miles north of downtown, and **William P. Hobby** about 10 miles southwest of downtown. If you are flying in, try to use the smaller and closer Hobby. Obviously with any city this size, lodgings in every price range and category are plentiful. Food options are endless and many are world class.

Day 21   Houston to Galveston

Distance *83 miles; 163 miles with the side trip*

Features *This short ride will get you out of the city. The rest of your day should be spent sightseeing at some of the many sites worthy of your attention, including the San Jacinto Monument, located on the battleground where Texas won her independence from Mexico; the Lyndon B. Johnson Space Center (NASA headquarters); and the famous Galveston historic district. If you want to ride more, take an 80-mile run along the scenic oceanfront out to the end of Galveston Island and back.*

The freeway system in and around Houston is not for the faint of heart. The traffic is heavy and the drivers are aggressive. Hang in there and stay alert as you navigate your way out of town. Starting at the intersection of I-45 and Loop 610 south of town, take Loop 610 east. After only two miles, take Exit 30B onto Hwy. 225 (La Porte Freeway) toward Pasadena. You will soon go through the towns of Pasadena and Deer Park. Most people are over-whelmed the first time through here by the sights and smells of the massive **crude oil refineries** and **petrochemical plants** that line this road. This area is the bedrock on which the Houston economy rests.

> **✪ *Alternate Route***
>
> If you need to put more mileage behind you today, you could skip the sightseeing (though I don't recommend it), and combine Day 21 and 22. From Houston, take I-45 out of the city and proceed directly to Galveston, about 45 miles away. From there, turn right on Seawall Blvd. and follow the directions for Day 22 from that point.

After 11 miles, exit onto Battleground Road (Hwy. 134) and follow signs to the **San Jacinto Monument.** Just 2-1/2 miles up this road, take a right to the battleground and monument. *Warning: If you choose not to make the pil-grimage to San Jacinto, you would be wise not to admit this to any Texan, lest you risk bodily injury or at least a good tongue-lashing.*

The **San Jacinto Historical Complex** is located on the site where the Texicans defeated **General Santa Anna** and his army on April 21, 1836, to secure their independence from Mexico. It was not much of a battle by to-day's standards: fewer than 1,000 Mexican soldiers were killed and only 9 Texicans.

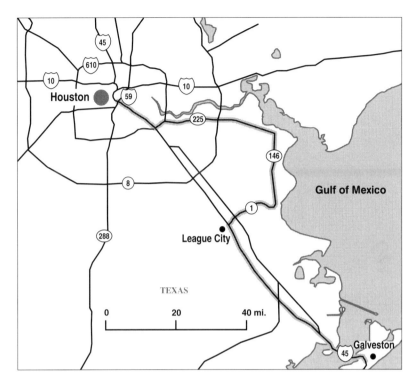

Attacking during the traditional *siesta* time, the Texicans were able to obtain complete surprise. The Mexicans reportedly attempted to surrender only 18 minutes into the battle, but the Texicans continued the killing for almost two hours shouting, "Remember the Alamo!" and "Remember Goliad!" Rumor has it that when the battle commenced, Santa Anna was being distracted by a mulatto slave woman who'd been sneaked into the Mexican camp. It's hard to lead troops with your pants down. The song, The Yellow Rose of Texas commemorates her contribution to Texan independence.

The battleground is marked by a 570-foot limestone obelisk said to be tallest in the world, 15 feet taller than the Washington Monument. An elevator can take you to an observation deck from which you can get a good view of what remains lovingly preserved of the original battleground—surrounded by Houston's industrial complexes, downtown bustle, and ship channel. A museum outlines early Texas history and shows a short film, *Texas Forever!* narrated by **Charlton Heston,** which expounds upon the events that took place here.

Leaving the battleground, follow the signs directing you to the permanent mooring of **the battleship Texas,** the last surviving battleship to serve in

The San Jacinto Monument marks the location of the battle where Texas won her independence from Mexico.

both World War I and World War II. It has been extensively renovated and is open for tours. From the battleship you can get a close look at the huge tankers carrying crude oil, petroleum products, and petrochemicals in and out of the ship channel.

After your visit to the San Jacinto Complex, retrace your route on Hwy. 134 to the intersection with Hwy. 225 and turn left. After 4 miles, turn right (south) onto 146. From this point, you will still be in an urban area, but the traffic thins to some extent and you can give your nerves a rest. After 9 miles take a right onto NASA Road 1 in Clear Lake. If you go over the huge bridge into Kemah, you will have gone too far. **Clear Lake** offers a wonderful sheltered cove for yachts and boats of every description, with access to the Gulf of Mexico via **Galveston Bay.**

Six miles along NASA Road 1, you'll see the **Lyndon B. Johnson Space Center** on your right, mission control for all NASA space operations. To see the facility, you must first visit **Space Center Houston,** located on your right about a block past the NASA entranceway. Several interesting exhibits and films outline the U.S. space program, and some of the original spacecraft are on display, including the last one to land on the moon. You can even touch a real moon rock. Trams to the NASA facility itself operate on an almost continuous basis. You can visit mission control, check out the astronaut training complex, and examine a training mock-up of a space shuttle. Many people spend a whole day here.

NASA 1 is lined with great eating establishments, most of which have delicious fresh seafood. Note that places along this stretch do not exist to serve those of us on a budget. One place that not only serves great seafood, but also offers wonderful views of the boat traffic into and out of Clear Lake, is **Jimmy Walker's** in Kemah. Backtrack to Hwy. 146 and turn right across the bridge. The restaurant will be on your left as you leave the bridge.

The quickest and easiest way to reach your destination of **Galveston Island** is to continue on NASA 1 until the intersection with I-45. From there, you head south for approximately 28 miles until you cross the bridge onto the island. As you travel along this road, the traffic thins, and you will soon be in a rural area of vast marshlands. After crossing onto the island, the road becomes Broadway (Avenue J). Continue straight ahead until you reach the ocean.

Galveston does not put its best foot forward as you enter the city. You will pass through some fairly seedy neighborhoods. However, as you approach the ocean, the restored Victorian homes begin to brighten your view. When you can see the ocean, turn right, to put yourself on Seawall Blvd. (for some reason, this intersection is marked as 6th Street).

❍ *Side Trip*

If you have the time, you can continue on this road to the end of the island, about 40 miles away. The ride out and back is very straightforward and scenic, with lots of places to take in the ocean beaches and bayside marshes.

The city and island of **Galveston** have had a "boom and bust" history. Not much is known about its early inhabitants, as periodic hurricanes have destroyed any remains or artifacts. When the area was discovered by white men, the **Karankawa Indians** were living here, but it didn't take long before they were driven from their homeland to west Texas, where they died out. Both the Spanish and French made unsuccessful attempts to found permanent settlements. In 1817, the buccaneer **Jean Lafitte** established the pirate stronghold of **Campeachy,** but it lasted only four short years, though they were no doubt rough and rowdy times. Legends of buried treasure persist to this day.

During the Civil War, Galveston was captured by Union forces and then recaptured by the Confederates. After the war, Galveston became the most modern city in Texas and prospered as the nation's third-largest port and a major banking center. But everything changed on September 8, 1900, when a massive hurricane completely destroyed Galveston and killed an estimated

The Bishop's Palace in Galveston is just on of the many fine, old Victorian homes that have been restored in this city by the sea.

6,000 of its 36,000 residents. The ten-mile seawall we see today was built for protection, and the elevation of the city was raised almost 20 feet behind this seawall. Despite these measures, Galveston never recovered from this event, and shipping and business interests moved inland to Houston.

In the 1930s and '40s an attempt was made to revive the island's economy by making it into a gambling haven. Massive efforts by law enforcement shut down this illegal activity in the 1950s, as the city had become dangerous. By the 1960s, Galveston had carved a promising niche for itself as a port that primarily handled fruits and produce. Today, this is the base of the economy, with tourism a strong second. Another attraction to Galveston, other than its beaches and oceanfront, is the more than **1,500 restored Victorian homes,** 500 of which are on the National Historic Register.

There is a good selection of motels and hotels in Galveston in every price range. A good medium-priced place to stay is **Gaido's Seaside Inn** located at 3828 Seawall Blvd. ($60; 409-762-9626, 800-525-0064). As anywhere else, a room with an ocean view commands a premium; you can save about $10 if you don't mind a view of a parking lot. Note also that the fenced, locked parking area for these rooms is quieter and more secure than the one facing the seawall.

If budget is no problem, stay at the **Tremont House** at 2300 Mechanic Street ($100+; 409-763-0300), an 1800s building that was converted to a luxury hotel in the 1980s with no expense spared. It contains a nice court-yard and rooftop bar from which you can enjoy the sunset.

Gaido's restaurant, next to the inn, is deemed by many to be the best place to eat on the island. Run by the same family for more than 85 years, they serve up huge portions of great seafood. Nevertheless, this place can be pricey and you might not be comfortable in your casual clothes. **Casey's Seafood Restaurant,** located in the motel, has the same fare at a much lower price, as it has the same owners and operators as Gaido's.

The nearest camping to the city of Galveston is about 6 miles southwest off Seawall Blvd., on 61st Southeast at **Galveston Island State Park** ($15; 409-737-1222). This is a beautiful setting with nature trails that go from the ocean on one side to the bay on the other. The oceanside camping is usually more crowed; the remote bay side can get pretty hot and buggy on a still night. If you wish, there are a limited number of screened shelters available each night for a few dollars more. If you are really lucky you will be there when a Broadway musical is being preformed in its outdoor theater. Galveston State Park accepts reservations and the facilities include flush toilets, showers, grills, and picnic tables. Turn left at the sign to get your space assigned and pay before settling in.

The **Galveston Convention and Visitors Bureau** at 2106 Seawall offers an amazing array of brochures on things to do and see on the island. If you are interested in touring the many Victorian homes in comfort, a trolley will take you through the **Strand** and **Silk Stocking,** two of the historic districts. The cost is only $1 and you can park your bike at the center.

To get an idea of how the rich of Galveston lived during its heyday, visit **The Grand,** the opera house built in 1894. Located at 2020 Post Office, it is a magnificent building. Self-guided tours are available of the interior. **Sarah Bernhardt, Paderewski, Anna Pavlova, John Philip Sousa, Helen Hayes,** and the **Vienna Boys Choir** are among those who have performed here. It is true opulence.

The **Bishop's Palace,** located at 1402 Broadway, will be on your left as you enter Galveston. The **American Institute of Architecture** has designated this Victorian structure as the second most impressive in the United States. It was built in 1886 at an estimated cost of $250,000 by **Colonel Walter Gresham.** In 1923, it was purchased by the Galveston-Houston Diocese as a home for the late **Bishop Christopher Byrne,** thereby gaining the name of Bishop's Palace. After the bishop's death in 1950 it was opened to the public. Original in every detail and carefully preserved, tours are offered daily. If you plan to see only one of these homes, this one is it.

Day 22   Galveston to Rockport

Distance *210 miles*

Features *Miles of riding along the south Texas coast, an opportunity to ride your bike on the beach, views of massive petrochemical plants, and a visit to one of the largest and most interesting wildlife preserves in the world will make this an interesting and full day.*

From your hotel in Galveston, ride west on Seawall Blvd. You will soon leave the built-up zone of city services and find yourself passing by numerous beach homes built atop stilts. The area then quickly turns to open sand dunes and marshland. After roughly six miles, **Galveston Island State**

This "jack-up" drilling rig is ready to find some more of that "Texas Tea."

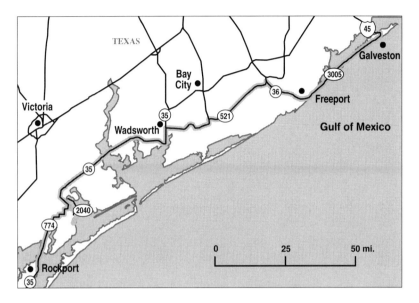

Park straddles the entire island. The park headquarters on the left is a good place to get off the bike and take a stroll on the beach to enjoy the fresh sea breezes. If you turn right here, there is a nice, short loop through the marshes to the bay with campers and RVs dotted about.

At the end of the Galveston Island you'll have to pay a $2 toll to cross over the **San Luis Pass Bridge** onto **Follets Island.** From there, the next 13 miles to the resort town of **Surfside Beach** is a beautiful ride along the ocean. At several points, you can access the beach with your motorcycle and once there, you can amble along with the sea lapping at your wheels. Most of the access points consist of good hardpack, but you should probably avoid the ones where you can see loose sand before reaching the beach. The beach surface between the high and low tide marks is good and many motorcyclists and automobiles travel it everyday. This place is almost deserted during the week and has very few people on it even on the weekends.

At the traffic light you should take a right onto Hwy. 332. Keep your eye out as you approach this light as there are usually **giant offshore drilling rigs,** known as "jack–up" rigs. You can ride up to them and see just how big and complicated these monsters are.

After crossing over the bridge to the mainland, you will enter the town of **Freeport,** a heavily industrialized area thick with petrochemical plants. At the first traffic light, turn left onto Hwy. 523 (a sign also points to Hwy. 36). Continue to work your way through this developed area following signs to Hwy. 36. After about 7 miles, Hwy. 36 takes off to the right at the yellow

Shrimping is a major industry along the Gulf Coast of Texas. The fleet works at night and rests during the day. It doesn't get any fresher than this! (photo by Jack Lewis/TxDOT)

flashing light. It is obvious that Hwy. 36 was built by dredging the marshes. As a result, it has nice stretches of water along both sides. Many people will be fishing or casting nets in an attempt to catch the bounty contained therein.

Soon you will cross the **Intracoastal Waterway** and gradually gain a small amount of altitude. As you do this, the marshland gives way to woods and an occasional farm. After about 16 miles, turn left onto Hwy. 521. The next 28 miles makes for a very pleasant ride through lush vegetation with many stream crossings and pecan groves. While this road is primarily straight, there are quite a few S-curves scattered along to keep your attention.

At the T-intersection with Hwy. 60 in Wadsworth, Hwy. 521 goes to the left, and after a very short distance, leaves Hwy. 60 to the right; stay on Hwy. 521. The landscape for the next 21 miles will consist of huge farms reaching as far as the eye can see. The most dramatic feature along this ride, a **nuclear power plant** with high-voltage power lines stretching to the horizon, has a nice roadside stop explaining its history and operation. Guided tours are also available.

From this point, turn left onto Hwy. 35 and continue 5 miles to the small town of **Palacious** (pop. 4,500). This small town lives on because an enormous fishing fleet calls this home. Seafood processing plants here get the catch ready for market. To get a good look at the fleet as you come into town, take Hwy. 35 Business and then turn left at the sign indicating the public boat ramp. At the end of the street that runs along he bay, retrace your route and make a left onto Hwy. 35 Business to continue on your way. Hwy. 35 Business shortly rejoins Hwy. 35 where you should turn left (south). The next few miles offer attractive views of the many bays along which the road runs.

After approximately 26 miles you will cross over a long bridge and enter the town of **Port Lavaca.** As one would assume while traveling along a stretch of road bordering on the gulf, you can get good, fresh seafood in every town. Just after leaving the bridge in Port Lavaca, however, there's a place on your right that is unusual for the area. **Gordon's Seafood Grill** doesn't look like much from the road, but the interior is very upscale and the seafood is prepared in an epicurean fashion. If you desire something other than the usual fried or boiled fish, shrimp, or crab, try this place. Be forewarned—it is somewhat pricey.

Continue on Hwy. 35 south for about 23 miles and make a left turn onto Hwy. 239 in Maudlowe. The first few miles of this run pass through farmland and then becomes marshier. There are many wildlife preserves through here which resemble the Florida Everglades.

Sights such as these bring birders from around the world to south Texas. (photo by TxDOT)

The whooping crane population is making a nice comeback wintering in the Aransas Park Wildlife Refuge and co-existing with the oil industry nearby. (photo by TxDOT)

The turns to the **Aransas Pass Wildlife Refuge** are well-marked: after about 4 miles, Hwy. 239 ends in the small town of Austwell. Make a right turn onto Hwy. 774. Continue for one mile and then turn left onto Hwy. 2040. After seven miles of riding on this increasingly narrow road, with the terrain growing swampy, you will find yourself at the park headquarters. Aransas is the winter home of the **whooping crane,** which is making a slow comeback from near extinction. The estimated worldwide population of these birds in 1945 was 15; the present count numbers more than 400. Five miles into the preserve there is an observation tower that allows one to look out over part of the park's 59,000 acres.

If you wish, you may return to the entrance via an eleven-mile one-way paved road through the backlands, which gives you an opportunity to see close-up the varying landscapes that make up this wonderful place. Please honor the 15 and 25 mph speed limits as the park is inhabited by deer, javelinas, bobcats, raccoons, alligators, turtles, frogs, snakes, and hundreds of bird species. The deer have become especially accustomed to the traffic and you may find the road around any curve completely blocked. If you plan to take any of the many hiking trails or spend a good deal of time off your bike, pick up some bug repellant at headquarters.

Leaving the refuge, retrace your route to the intersection with Hwy. 774 and make a left turn. While this road proceeds mostly flat and straight through farmland, it does have a few unmarked 90-degree turns along its nine miles. Stay alert. Turn left onto Hwy. 35 south at the intersection and proceed approximately 13 miles to the left turn on Park Road 13 into **Goose Island State Park.** At the STOP sign, go straight ahead. This small road meanders around and then goes to the left along the seaside.

As the road turns left away from the ocean, the **Big Tree,** also known as the Lamar Oak or the Bishop Oak, will be on your right. The largest oak tree in Texas, it has a circumference of 35 feet, stands 44 feet tall, and has a crown of 89 feet. It is estimated to be more than 1,000 years old, and sitting as it does right on the gulf, one can only wonder how many hurricanes it has survived.

After your visit, continue on the small road through the oak groves, turning left at the T-intersection, and right at the four-way stop. Then retrace your route to Hwy. 35 where you should turn left. This little loop down to see the tree is only 2 or 3 miles and will not take much time.

If you are camping, sites are available in the **Goose Tree State Park** itself, with almost all the services you will need for a wonderful night nestled in a live oak forest. There is no food here, however. If you prefer to be in a more urban setting, continue on to Rockport to the **Ancient Oaks RV Park** located at 1222 Hwy. 35 south; their facilities include a laundry room, fishing pier, and swimming pool.

After 13 or so more miles on Hwy. 35, you will come to a long bridge spanning **Copano Bay.** Another 3 miles will bring you to a left turn onto Fulton Beach Road. You will soon be running along the seafront with modern condominiums sharing the area with several old mansions.

A more than adequate "mom and pop" place to stay is the **Bayfront Cottages** located next to the Fulton Mansion ($45; 512-729-6693). Should you prefer more modern accommodations, continue to the intersection with Hwy. 35 and turn left into Rockport proper where you will find all the national chains represented. There are plenty of good places to eat, but for a unique treat, try the **Boiling Pot** located on Fulton Beach Road at Palmetto Street. Shrimp, crab, and raw fish are boiled in water rich with Cajun spices and then deposited directly onto your paper-covered table for your further handling. For an extra treat, try a cup of the gumbo.

The cities of **Rockport** and **Fulton,** separated in name only, abut each other with no noticeable boundaries. With a combined population of approximately 7,000, the mainstay of the local economy is fishing. Originally developed by the **Morgan Steamship Company** as a port for shipping Texas

Fishing attracts many to the Gulf Coast of Texas. Stroll out on one of the numerous piers and ask, "How are they biting today?"

It should come as no surprise to learn where they found the rocks to build this mansion. (photo by Bill Reaves/TxDOT)

beef to the northeast, the advent of the railroad put it into a quick decline. The old mansions along the coast are the only reminders of the glory days. The **Fulton Mansion State Historical Structure,** located on Fulton Beach Road just after entering the Rockport city limits, is the most magnificent of the examples. Built in the 1870s by a cattle baron, it has been restored in all its grandeur. Guided tours are available to show you around and explain the history and uniqueness of this home.

These days, Rockport considers itself the premier **artists' colony** in Texas and many galleries showcase the local wares. Tourism is also becoming more and more important, and all the usual beach activities are well represented. If you want to see more of the **Aransas Wildlife Refuge,** several boat tours leave regularly from the beachfront.

Day 23   Rockport to Port Isabel

Distance *220 miles*

Features *This day offers yet more chances to explore beautiful south Texas beaches, visit some small fishing villages, and travel through the vast farmlands that make this the breadbasket of Texas and much of the nation. You can check out the world's largest ranch and the town that grew from it. The day ends either in a picturesque fishing village, or a modern world-class beach resort town, as you wish.*

From downtown Rockport, continue south on Hwy. 35 for approximately 8 miles and make a left onto Loop 90 to Port Aransas and to Hwy. 361. When you come to the intersection with Hwy. 361, take a left and proceed 7 more miles to the ferry crossing onto Mustang Island. The five-minute ferry ride is free and operates 24 hours a day. After departing the ferry, you should take the first right and continue on Hwy. 361 for approximately 18 miles to the intersection with Park Road 22 on the outskirts of Corpus Christi.

You will know that you are in tropical Texas as you ride these palm-tree lined roads. (photo by Jack Lewis/ TxDOT)

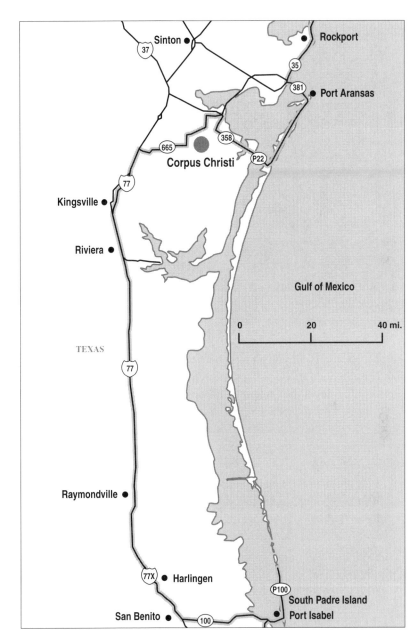

Virtually undeveloped except for the small town of **Port Aransas** in the
north, **Mustang Island** has some of the best beaches in Texas. Historically,
the fishing village was very difficult to get to, and this suited the locals just
fine. With the extension of Hwy. 361 a few years back, this place became

Corpus Christi, a booming petrochemical town and seaport, still has wonderful beaches nearby. (photo by Jack Lewis/TxDOT)

much more accessible and a few condos appeared at the south end of town, but it hasn't yet lost its laid-back beach lifestyle.

Hwy. 361 down the center of Mustang Island splits through the rolling sand dunes covered with sea oats. You can ride your motorcycle on the beach, but yesterday's caveats still apply.

✪ Side Trip

At the intersection with Park Road 22 you can take a left and run about 5 miles on a paved road to the **Padre Island National Seashore Visitors' Center,** which contains interesting exhibits regarding the world's longest coastal barrier island (113 miles). The pavement extends only about a mile past the center, but you can then continue on the beach if you want. Be aware, however, that the riding surface soon deteriorates and becomes impassable after about 5 miles.

After your visit to Padre Island, return out of the park on Park Road 22 and connect with Hwy. 358 into Corpus Christi (straight ahead). This highway soon becomes four-lane and then a major freeway traversing this city.

Corpus Christi is a thriving town with a population estimated at more than 300,000. It grew up as a raunchy port city, first known for its smuggling activities, and later for its bars, strip clubs, and the associated businesses that served the sailors and naval pilots based here. It has outgrown this image and is now a major port and home base for vast oil refining and processing industry. Corpus Christi is not known as a tourist destination, but rather as a jumping off point to the areas around it. The most popular attraction here is retired carrier, the **USS Lexington,** located on the ship channel at 2914 N. Shoreline Blvd. This carrier served in WWII and was on active duty until 1962 when it became a training ship. When it was retired from service in 1991, the city purchased it and moved it here. If you have never been on one of these ships, you will be astonished by its size.

Approximately 18 miles after getting on Hwy. 358, exit the freeway and turn left onto Hwy. 665 (Old Brownsville Road). Once you get onto Hwy. 665, you quickly leave the city behind for farmland. For the next 21 miles this road is flat and straight, though you have to make a clearly marked right turn at one point to continue on it. A few stiff curves occur here and there, but they are all marked with yellow flashing lights. When you intersect with Hwy. 77 in the town of Driscoll, turn left. After approximately 13 miles of straight, high-speed road, take a right onto King Street (Hwy. 141) in Kingsville.

Massive amounts of oil and associated riches are still being produced in much of south Texas today. This will be a common sight along your ride.

Unless you're looking for a job, be sure and take a left as you approach the entrance to the King Ranch.

Kingsville, the only town in the county of Kleberg, is the home of the world famous King Ranch. Founded by Rio Grande riverboat captain **Richard King** in 1853, the ranch now has holdings in Texas exceeding 1.2 million acres (the base ranch here, 825,000 acres, is larger than the state of Rhode Island). Currently owned by more than 100 of Captain King's heirs, the **King Ranch** operates as a multi-national corporation with worldwide holdings exceeding four million acres. The first American breed of beef cattle, the **Santa Gertrudis,** was established on the King Ranch, and its horse breeding has produced several Derby winners.

As luck would have it, the King Ranch also was sitting on a pool of oil, and this industry has become yet another important part of the Kingsville economy. Today, with a population of almost 30,000, Kingsville has a branch of **Texas A&M University** and a **naval air station.** If you are hungry, try **Los Amigos Restaurant** at 1920 E. King. It has a daily all-you-can-eat buffet featuring some of the finest Tex-Mex food you will ever encounter.

From the intersection of Hwys. 146 and 77 on the east side of Kingsville, head south. Be sure you have plenty of fuel and water, as the next 70 miles or so offer no services. From Kingsville, it is 103 miles of high-speed road to the turn-off onto Hwy. 100. The first 70 miles through chaparral and scrub will give you an idea of just how empty much of Texas really is. Even when you top a small hill, there will be no sign of man for as far as the eye can see in any direction.

This road turns into freeway as it works through the built-up areas of Harlingen and San Benito. Exit onto Hwy. 100 and turn left toward Port Isabel. You are now only 25 miles from the most famous and best-developed beaches in Texas, South Padre Island. The high-rise condominiums on the island are visible on the horizon many miles before you get to them. Take the two-mile long bridge that connects Port Isabel with South Padre Island and make the first left turn. All the upscale hotel chains have property here and it seems the condos run for miles. There's everything you can imagine in a top-notch resort destination: you can buy a T-shirt, get a tattoo, rent a dune buggy or motorcycle, parasail, jet ski, or charter a fishing or sail boat. There is even a gambling boat that goes out for evening cruises.

Tonight you have the option to stay either on South Padre Island, as described above, or in Port Isabel. If you choose **South Padre Island,** let your budget be your guide. By getting off the beach only a block or two, you'll find major chains, like **Motel 6** and **Days Inn** with rooms in the $35–40 range (these prices can double or triple during high season, on the weekends, or during special events). The rapid increase in land values and new development has left very few "mom and pop" places on the island. Most of these rent cottage-type accommodations with kitchens to families spending their annual week-long vacation on the beach. Campers will find the **Isla Blanca County Park** (956-761-5493) located on the south end of the island to be handy to the action.

Port Isabel is a much older and more picturesque town than South Padre Island. Although it has more permanent inhabitants (5,000 vs. 2,000) it lacks hordes of tourists. The **Port Isabel Lighthouse State Historic Structure,** on your left at the end of town near the bridge entrance, is hard to miss. Once a vital navigational aide to mariners, the lighthouse is still in operation today. It is open to visitors and the view from the top is grand, overlooking the development on South Padre Island and the surrounding waterways.

Port Isabel has several motels in the moderate to inexpensive range. The **Yacht Club Hotel** at 700 Yturria Street ($50; 956-943-1301) has great ambiance, as it is a restored 1920s fishing lodge. Dining options are plentiful and there is no shortage of great seafood. The dining room at the Yacht Club Hotel, considered the best place in town, offers the sort of upscale dishes that one would not expect to encounter in a town this size. It is reasonably expensive, but the cost is offset somewhat by the fact that your room rate includes a continental breakfast.

Day 24   Port Isabel to Laredo

Distance *235 miles*

Features *This day is a real mixed bag of riding, starting out with a run along the seashore, you'll soon be heading through the immense farmlands of the Rio Grande Valley. The day ends with miles of open spaces covered with mesquite, cactus, and scrubs. Take the time to visit an old Spanish mission and view what was once the northernmost port on the Rio Grande.*

At the intersection of Hwy. 48 with Hwy. 100 in Port Isabel, turn left onto Hwy. 48 toward Brownsville. This stretch is unusual in that on your left will be sand dunes covered with sea oats—a typical beachfront road; on your right, however, will be a desert landscape of cactus and scrub. It is as if the road serves as a climatic barrier.

Continue on Hwy. 48 for 23 miles. The road will become a four-laner as you approach Brownsville and it can get quite congested during rush hours; after you go under I-77, traffic will clear out some. At the intersection with Hwy. 281, continue straight (do not turn onto Hwy. 281 Business).

Your proximity to the Mexican border and the high percentage of Hispanic residents in the area is evident in the fact that almost all outdoor adver-

In south Texas, a little Spanish can come in handy.

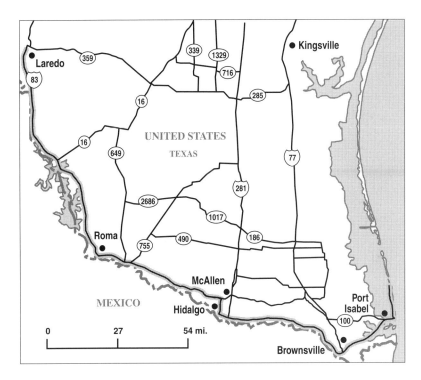

tising is in Spanish. In fact, Brownsville has more Spanish TV channels than English ones.

The next 50 miles or so on Hwy. 281 run through the heart of the **Rio Grande Valley** with its enormous farms being worked by migrant laborers. Climatic conditions produce a year-round growing season. The highway, a major truck route that conveys goods from Mexico, is a good, high-speed road that curves gently as it roughly follows the route of the **Rio Grande River.**

Just before the town of Hidalgo, the signs indicate a right turn onto Hwy. 281 north; do not make this turn, but continue straight ahead as the road turns into Hwy. 281 west. About two miles past this intersection, turn right onto Hwy. 336. To stay out of the congestion of McAllen, turn left onto Hwy. 1016 after about 4 miles. You will now find yourself riding through sugar cane and sorghum fields.

✪ *Side Trip*

Approximately 6 miles down Hwy. 1016, turn left at the sign for **La Lomita Mission.** Just a few hundred yards down the road, the

Are we in Texas or Mexico?

right turn to the mission will be clearly marked. Cross the railroad tracks and make a left. The mission will be ahead on your right in a small grove of oak and mesquite trees.

The **La Lomita Chapel** is located in a small, restful park. It was originally built in 1865 as an adobe overnight waystation for padres traveling between Brownsville and Roma. This tiny structure was rebuilt in 1889 of sandstone. Today it has been carefully restored and contains the original brick floor and heavy overhead wooden beams made from the nearby trees. A beehive oven and the well are also still in existence. Today the place is still used for special events, such as weddings, and locals come here to pray and light candles. When you are ready to return to the road, retrace your route and turn left when you intersect with Hwy. 1016.

Only two short miles down the road from the La Lomita turn-off, turn right onto Hwy. 83. The next 50 miles to Roma Los Saenz is all four-lane and you can make good speed through this fertile valley of aloe vera, onions, cabbage, and various other vegetables. From that point, you will come upon mile after mile of rolling chaparral thick with mesquite trees and prickly pear cactus. In Roma, turn left at the traffic light just past Lino's Pharmacy.

These days, **Roma** is just a sleepy border town, but from 1850 to 1900 it was the westernmost point on the Rio Grande open to steamboats. It was vital to the South during the Civil War as an export point for cotton. The left turn described above will get you down to the river and into the heart of the historic district, which contains **more than 38 restored structures.** Since it so well resembles a typical small Mexican town of the era, the outdoor scenes for the movie *Viva Zapata* were shot here. After visiting the river and the historic district, return to Hwy. 83 and turn left.

From this point, Hwy. 83 turns into a two-laner and traffic really drops off. The terrain becomes hillier and from the tops of the rises you can see forever over the mesquite—and cactus—covered countryside. The 40-mile run to the town of **Zapata** is about as desolate as it gets in the United States. If you love moving along open road on two wheels, this will be pure heaven. If you need fuel, tank up in Zapata, since the 48 miles to Laredo consist of more of this wonderfully deserted country.

As you approach Laredo, Hwy. 83 reverts to four-lanes, makes a quick 90-degree turn to the left and becomes Guadalupe Street. Continue onward toward Salinas and turn left at the blue sign that indicates TOURISTS TO MEXICO. Turn left on Lincoln Street, and in two blocks you will see the visitors' center on your left at the corner of Lincoln and St. Augustine. I recommend you stop here to pick up brochures and maps of the **Laredo Historic Dis-**

In south Texas, fine examples of old Spanish missions remain in active service today.

trict and information on visiting Mexico, as well as discount coupons for some of the hotels in the area.

If at all possible, consider spending two nights in Laredo so you can really experience this very interesting place. For a real treat, try the **La Posada Hotel & Suites** at 1000 Zaragoza Street (956-722-1701; 800-444-2099). The standard prices begin at $100 a night, but the last time I was through here, the visitors' center had coupons for a $69 rate. Sitting on the Rio Grande River, this hacienda-style hotel has nice courtyards filled with vegetation and flowers. It is located between the two international bridges and is within easy walking distance to both the historic district of Laredo and the tourist district of Nuevo Laredo. Some of the higher-priced rooms have patios overlooking the river into Mexico.

The quaint La Lomita Chapel sits in a restful grove of live oaks near McAllen. Established in 1865, it still is in service today.

Walking the streets of many small Texas towns today will make you feel as if you are on a western movie set. (photo by Bob Parvin/TxDOT)

I can't recommend the lower-priced hotels and motels in downtown Laredo. If you are seeking reasonably priced accommodations, head north on I-35 and you will find several "budget" chains, including a **Motel 6** ($45). The only camping in the Laredo area is in **Lake Casa Blanca State Park.** As the name would imply, the campsites are on the lake. Three options exist: sites without water, sites with water, and screened sites. To get here, take I-35 north to the Hwy. 59 east exit. Stay on Hwy. 59 and the park will be on your left just past the airport.

Laredo is a city of approximately 180,000 people, 90 percent of whom are Hispanic. The language heard most often on the streets and markets is a mixture of Spanish and English called "Spanlish." Laredo's economy revolves around trade between the United States and Mexico, and it is the largest port of entry between the two countries. With the advent of NAFTA and

Migrant laborers play a major role in harvesting the vast fields of produce in the Rio Grand Valley. (photo by Tx/DOT)

the subsequent *maquiladora* factories, Laredo has become the second-fastest growing city in the country (Las Vegas is first).

For the visitor, Laredo consists of the downtown historic district. You will feel you as if you are south of the border, with street vendors hawking traditional Mexican foods from their carts, walkways cluttered with wares, and rampant bargaining.

Located right next to La Posada Hotel & Suites is the **Republic of the Rio Grande Museum,** which has exhibits concerning the short period of time after the Texas War of Independence that the Laredo area was an independent republic. From here, you can catch an air-conditioned trolley tour of the rest of the historical district, sit back, relax, and let a guide explain what you are seeing. A brochure at the visitors' center also outlines a walking tour of the historic district. The oldest section of Laredo is around **San Augustín Plaza,** just across Zaragoza Street from the hotel. Several cobblestone walkways leading from it provide welcome shade and places to just sit and watch the goings on.

Just a short stroll across **International Bridge #1,** you enter into Mexico and the city of **Nuevo Laredo.** You don't need any paperwork to go over and spend the day, as long as you have a photo ID. As you enter Mexico, the road becomes Guerrero Avenue and the next nine blocks along this busy street to **Plaza Hidalgo** will really give you a feel for the differences, as well as the similarities, of these twin cities. Nuevo Laredo is the larger of the two, with an estimated population of 400,000.

Be sure to stop in the **Mercado Juárez** on your right, just after Calle Belden, to see a typical Mexican market in operation. As a general rule, the closer you are to the border, the more expensive the food will be, as these establishments are geared to the tourist trade. On the south side of Plaza Hildalgo, the **Café Lanchería** serves up Mexican (not Tex-Mex) dishes at reasonable prices. As always in Mexico, drink only bottled beverages. The merchants in Nuevo Laredo usually accept U.S. dollars, but it is fun to change a few dollars into pesos at the bridge so you can use the local currency. You can change back any leftover pesos on your return.

The fertile Rio Grande valley provides much of the citrus found in your local supermarket. Here you can "pick it up at the factory." (photo by Richard Reynolds/TxDOT)

The old lighthouse in Port Isabel still leads ships home. It is a very popular motorcycling destination and the view from the top is extraordinary. (courtesy of TxDOT)

PORT ISABEL LIGHTHOUSE
STATE HISTORIC STRUCTURE
TEXAS PARKS & WILDLIFE DEPARTMENT

A few words of caution: As with border towns everywhere, petty crime here is fairly high, though if you are alert, you should have no problems. Authorities in both cities understand the value of the tourist trade, and as a result, violent crime is almost non-existent. That said, avoid carrying large sums of cash in the historic district of Laredo and the tourist district of Nuevo Laredo and do not walk along unlit streets at night. Park your bike in a secure area with 24-hour protection.

During your visit to Nuevo Laredo, you will likely encounter people on the street offering to sell you all sorts of goods and services, some legal, some not. Try to remember that these folks are usually just trying to make a living the only way they can. A grin and a friendly, "No, gracias," should be enough to send them on to the next prospect. Should you ever feel uncom-

This is a common sight along the Texas-Mexico border . . . an impossible task.

fortable, just walk over to one of the many policemen who will be around and tell him of your problem.

Do not under *any circumstances* carry a weapon, or even ammunition into Mexico, unless you would enjoy a lengthy stay in a Mexican jail. Knives are considered weapons, and it is best to leave your pocketknife in your hotel room. For some excellent tips to make your crossing painless, pick up the Crossing Guide for Los Dos Laredos, a brochure available at the visitors' center. Go and enjoy the experience!

Day 25   Laredo to Goliad

Distance *200 miles*

Features *Leaving the rugged terrain of south central Texas, you will encounter farmlands and pass through several oil fields with their associated equipment dotting the landscape. As you approach Goliad, the landscape becomes wetter and more lush with trees and vegetation. Since tomorrow will be a full day of riding, try to get to Goliad in time for some sightseeing this afternoon.*

Since the first part of today's ride is through some fairly desolate country, be sure your tank is topped off and you have a good supply of water with you before you depart the city. From San Augustín Plaza, head north on any street until you reach Chihuahua Street and then turn right (this runs parallel to your route into the city, but in the opposite direction). The street will make a 90-degree turn to the right and become Hwy. 83. Just after this point, take a left onto Hwy. 359.

The Empressario restaurant in the small town of Goliad is the place.

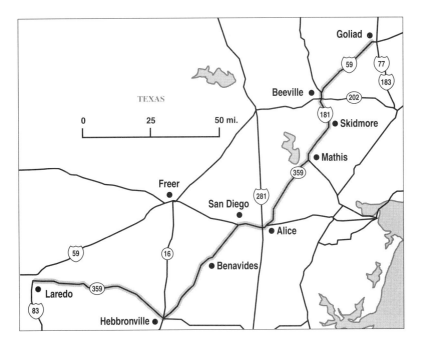

After you depart the outskirts of Laredo, you will find yourself again in open country. The road has gentle hills and an occasional sweeper that seems to last for miles. After approximately 43 miles, you'll reach the town of Hebbronville, where Hwy. 359 makes a right turn, and then an almost immediate left turn, and one block later another left turn (all of which are clearly marked). It is now approximately 65 miles to the town of Alice. Just follow Hwy. 359 signs through the virtual ghost town of Benavides and make the clearly marked right turn in San Diego. Enjoy these miles, as after this you will be back into "civilization."

When you arrive in **Alice** (pop. 20,000) you will have left the brush country to the west and re-entered the coastal plains. Alice is located only 29 road-miles from Kingsville and was named after one of Captain King's daughters. From 1888 to 1985 it was the world's largest cattle shipping point. Oil was discovered in the area in the 1930s and remains the primary business today. Alice is considered the dividing line between the border regions and the rest of Texas. Hwy. 359 takes off to the left in Alice, and you will be on a rural, two-lane road again.

Hwy. 359 runs through mostly farm and pasture lands for the 26 miles to Mathis, where you will begin to see trees again. This area produces large quantities of grain sorghum, flax, and oil. Follow the signs for Hwy. 359 in Mathis and continue onward. Should you wish to get a taste of Africa, make

The Presidio La Bahia in Goliad makes for an interesting visit to explore Texas roots.

a stop at **Wayne's World Safari,** located about one and one-half miles on Hwy. 359, after the intersection with I-37. Covering over 50 acres, this wildlife park contains more than 300 animals, including tigers, bears, lions, zebras, monkeys, and many more species, all roaming freely on the plains.

Continue on Hwy. 359 for approximately 13 more miles and turn left onto Hwy. 181 north in the town of Skidmore. The next 12 miles of four-lane road present a very dramatic change in scenery. Turn right off Hwy. 181 in Beeville onto Hwy. 59 toward Goliad. As you ride the 28 miles to Goliad, the terrain becomes hillier and the road has a few interesting curves. More and more, as the roadside becomes more forested, you will realize that you have left the coast behind.

As you enter Goliad, the **Antlers Inn** ($40; 512-645-8215) will be on your right. This is the best place to stay in town, although there is another budget motel ahead at the light. There are several fast food options and the **Hunter's Café** at the hotel serves adequate food. By far the best place to eat in town is the **Empresario Restaurant** located on the town square. Unfortunately, it is open for dinner only Thursday through Saturday nights. To get to the square, follow signs for the historic district, with its historical markers and old buildings. A huge oak tree, known as **"the hanging tree,"** earned its moniker during the years following the Civil War, when a group of men known as The Regulators filled the vacuum left behind by a lack of organized law enforcement. With no trials, justice was swift and the sentences were predetermined by these men.

Campers should continue to the intersection with Hwy. 77 Alternate/183 and turn right. About two miles down this road, the **Goliad State Park** will be on your right, with both primitive and improved sites, as well as toilets and shower facilities.

The small town of **Goliad** (pop. 2,000) sits among live oak groves on the banks of the **San Antonio River.** One of the oldest settlements in Texas, it recently celebrated its 250th birthday. While it is now just a sleepy little ranching town, it was once a major cattle center larger than San Antonio. As Galveston gained ground as the main port in Texas, Goliad declined. Hollywood has ensured that most people are familiar with the Texican battle cry, "Remember the Alamo!" but an event that took place in Goliad was actually an even more stirring factor in fueling Texican resolve to win independence from Mexico.

The sleepy little Texas towns you will encounter during this ride will make you think of stopping and staying a spell.

These shaded roads cast a very different picture of Texas after you've spent a few days in the wide-open spaces.

After the defeat at the Alamo, Texican colonel **James Fannin** was ordered to withdraw his troops from the fort in Goliad and join up with Sam Houston's forces in the east. Shortly after leaving the fort, Fannin and his men encountered a superior Mexican force and surrendered honorably as prisoners of war. On March 27, 1836 (Palm Sunday), **General Santa Anna** ordered all 350 of these men to be executed by firing squad; the bodies were stripped and left unburied. Such an atrocity inflamed the Texicans, and when they encountered the enemy later at San Jacinto, the slaughter continued for more than two hours after Mexico attempted to surrender, accompanied by cries of, "Remember Goliad!"

The fort, **Presidio La Bahia** was originally established by the Spanish to protect the **Mision Nuestra Senora del Espirtu Santo de Zuniga,** which had become a major ranching center for Texas. Located just south of town on opposite banks of the San Antonio River, these two sites have been carefully restored and are open to the public. The fort, the size of a city block, is considered the best surviving example of the Spanish presidios. You are free to roam the interior and visit the small museum containing artifacts and other memorabilia from the Texas Revolution. Located in **Goliad State Park,** just across the river, the mission has also been restored and contains exhibits outlining the daily life of the padres and the Indian converts during its 110-year history as an active mission. To get to these sites, just go south out of town for about two miles on Hwy. 183/77 Alternate.

Day 26   Goliad to Houston

Distance *240 miles*

Features *This day offers a real contrast to everything you have experienced so far. Most of the day consists of hilly, curvy roads that can be ridden as aggressively as you want. The old town of Gonzales, the birthplace of Texas Independence, makes for a nice lunch stop. Your day ends with a high-speed run through miles of rice fields as you approach Houston.*

Much of this route follows Texas Independence Trail. Be sure to show proper respect.

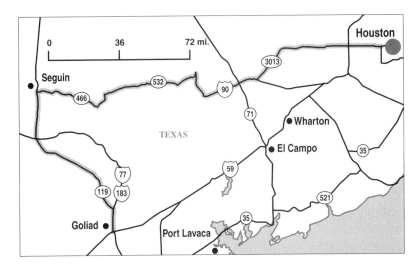

From the intersection of Hwys. 59 and 183/77 Alternate, head north toward Cuero on 183/77 Alternate for approximately 9 miles, and then turn left onto Hwy. 119. The next 58 miles are full of gently rolling hills and curves meandering through pastureland and live oak tree groves. Settled by people of European descent (mostly Lithuanians), there's relatively little evidence of Hispanic culture in the area.

As you come to the town of Stockdale, take a left onto Hwy. 87 at the T-intersection and about a quarter-mile later, turn right onto Hwy. 123. The next 20 miles or so consist of good high-speed riding on a somewhat larger road than before.

Turn right onto Hwy. 477. After about 2 miles, Hwy. 477 ends at the intersection with Hwy. 1117, and you should proceed straight to pick up Hwy. 466, which is part of the **Texas Independence Trail.** You can easily imagine settlers with horse-drawn wagons traversing this hilly landscape and camping along the sides of the streams. You may even have to reduce your speed to navigate the curves.

After approximately 27 miles of pure riding pleasure, turn left onto Hwy. 97. Go 5 miles, and then turn left onto Hwy. 183. In about 2 miles, take a right onto Hwy. 183 Business in Gonzales (the sign also indicates the historic district).

Known as the **"Lexington" of Texas,** the first shots fired in the War of Independence were discharged in Gonzales. When the Mexicans demanded that the townspeople give up their small cannon, they refused, and fought under a hastily made banner that said, "Come and Take It." Thirty-two men who made a mad dash to the Alamo to help in its defense lost their lives. As he began his retreat to San Jacinto, **Sam Houston** ordered the town evacuated and burned to the ground.

After the war, **Gonzales** was rebuilt and it became an important ranching area. Old cotton plantations and majestic homes line tree-lined boulevards. The old jail constructed in 1887 on the main square has been restored, complete with cells, dungeon, and gallows. The chamber of commerce located here can provide you with a map for a short ride around the town to see the more impressive old homes.

After visiting downtown Gonzales, continue on Hwy. 183 Business to the intersection with Hwy. 90 Alternate and turn right. Only 2 miles down this road, make a left turn onto Hwy. 532, which is a road any motorcyclist will enjoy. After about 18 miles on Hwy. 532, turn right in the town of Moulton, make another right as it joins Hwy. 95, and a left just a short way down this road, and then another left (all these turns are clearly marked).

Over the next 15 miles, the road opens up somewhat and you might be tempted to twist the throttle, as you have good visibility through the turns. Be on the lookout, as there are several 90-degree curves along here and if you are riding at high speed, they can sneak up on you. You should make a right turn as Hwy. 532 joins with Hwy. 77 for a short distance before leaving it to the left toward Oakland.

The banner says it all about the attitude of Texicans during the War of Independence from Mexico. If you want this cannon, "Come and take it!" (photo by Jack Lewis/TxDOT)

Large rice storage and transporting facilities sprout out of the otherwise flat marshlands as you approach the sprawl of Houston.

Turn right onto Hwy. 155 at the T-intersection. Eleven more miles will place you at the end of Hwy. 532, where you need to turn right onto Hwy. 155. The next 11 miles are on a major state highway through a vast rice growing region. There are several wildlife refuges through here and many migratory birds winter in the area. The small town of Eagle Lake is the self-proclaimed **Goose Hunting Capitol of the World.**

Shortly after passing through **Eagle Lake,** take a left onto Hwy. 3013, for a straight 17-mile shot to the intersection with Hwy. 36, where you should turn left. Take I-10 east just south of Sealy and 45 miles later you will be back in Houston at the intersection with Loop 610, an experience that will give you an appreciation for just how huge Houston has become—you will have passed through nearly 20 miles of ever-increasing development with subdivisions, shopping malls, and even some modest skyscrapers.

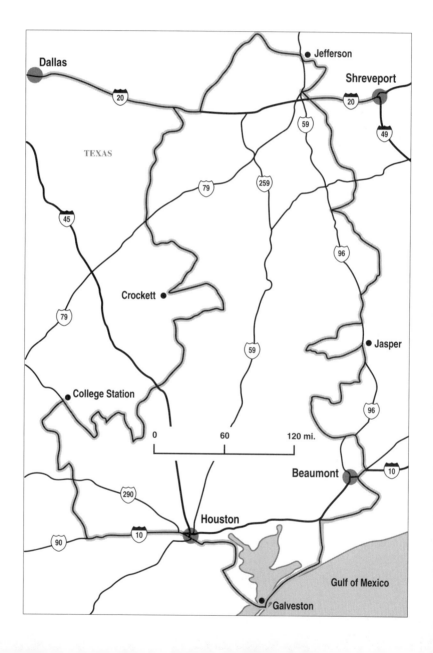

Dallas-Fort Worth East Texas

Forget any preconceived ideas you may have about Texas. East Texas is very different from the rest of the state, with an abundance of thick forests, rivers, bayous, and lakes. The flat coastal marshes and grasslands turn into gently rolling hills as you head north. This chapter details six days of riding, covering approximately 1,280 miles, starting and ending in Dallas. All the routes described here are paved, but the four national forests through which you will travel and the Big Thicket National Preserve contain a maze of dirt roads that offer hour after hour of backcountry riding.

Culturally, east Texas also moves to its own beat and you will see fewer folks in cowboy hats and boots. East Texas was primarily settled by people from the southeastern United States: cotton farmers and second sons of old families from Georgia, Alabama, and Mississippi. Since this was the only area of Texas to hold significant numbers of slaves, today's population has a larger percentage of blacks than other rural parts of the state. Its distance from Mexico has mitigated Texas's otherwise heavy Spanish heritage. Instead, the earliest history of Texas was influenced by the French; a Creole and Cajun heritage spilling from neighboring Louisiana still can be found in the local accents, food, and style.

From a rider's point of view, east Texas is a delight. Roads seem to go in every direction, twisting and turning through the forests and piney woods. Except for along the coast, this area is relatively undeveloped. The residents are more laid-back, and the abundant opportunities to enjoy regional food will more than likely put a few inches on your waist before you leave. The architecture of the buildings and homes in these small, scattered towns resembles that of New Orleans. Oil and lumber are the primary industries, though tourist dollars are helping to cultivate an appreciation for the unique history of the area.

Dallas-Fort Worth and the surrounding suburbs have the largest population of any area in Texas. From a standard metropolitan area measurement viewpoint, the "metroplex" contains more than 5,000,000 people. Dallas is the larger of the two cities, and can claim approximately 1,250,000 citizens within its limits. The Big D also has more shopping area per capita than any other city in the nation. These people like to spend their wealth and show it off. By comparison, Fort Worth (Cowtown, USA), with a mere 600,000 res-

Evidence of the oil industry will be all around you as you ride the Texas gulf coast. This semi-submersible drilling rig is headed for offshore waters to continue the search for resources and riches. (photo by Randy Green/ TxDOT)

idents, trails far behind in population. While Fort Worth has money in its own right, the people seem to care less about what the world thinks of them and are less ostentatious in their lifestyles.

Dallas was founded in 1840 on the **Trinity River** with the building of one log cabin that served as an area trading post. It slowly grew over the years, but ranching, farming and the usual small town Texas economy never developed. Trading remained the lifeblood of Dallas. In the early 1870s, two rail lines were extended to Dallas, and the town grew. Although cattle were not driven to Dallas, cattle futures were traded there. When oil money from other parts of Texas came to Dallas to be "put to work," the area became a center for banking and insurance. Today it is the home of many Fortune 500 companies, as well as a center for the high-tech and aviation industries. As a result of this diversity, Dallas considers its economy virtually "recession proof."

Fort Worth was established as an army camp in the 1850s, but a small g roup of settlers soon built cabins around the camp for protection from the Indians. After the Civil War, when the great cattle drives from Texas to Abilene, Kansas, began, Fort Worth was the last place to get provisions and supplies on the way north; heading back south, it was the first place the cowboys could spend their money and have a good time. Think of all those Westerns that depicted cowboys riding their horses up and down the streets shooting their guns in the air, drinking, gambling, whoring, and having just a generally rowdy time. This was Fort Worth.

When the railroad reached town in 1876, Fort Worth became the endpoint of the drives and vast cattle yards and feedlots were built. Gradually, over the years, improved transportation and refrigerated transport led to the construction of many packing plants here, and the need for the stockyards decreased. Today, Fort Worth has transformed itself into a fully modern city, and is the home of American Airlines, Bell Helicopter, Pier One Imports, and numerous other national and international companies.

With the exception of man-made "green belts" the Dallas-Fort Worth area sits on a vast plain with few trees. It is not a rider's dream. However, **DFW airport,** larger than the entire island of Manhattan, is one of the busiest in the world. Since flying into the Dallas area from anywhere in the world is easy, and rental bikes are available (see Appendix A2), I chose to start and end this chapter here. In a little more than 100 miles of high-speed riding, you will be enjoying wonderful roads through the piney woods of east Texas.

Both Dallas and Fort Worth can brag of world-class museums of all types, but there are some sights unique to these cities that you might care to visit:

Southfork Ranch. You can visit the location where the famous TV show *Dallas* was filmed in the '70s and '80s. This series was responsible for branding a whole generation with the notion that Texans and Texas oilmen were as devious as **J.R. Ewing,** with his "anything is O.K. for me, because I am rich" attitude. Today the site displays memorabilia, including "the gun that shot J.R." It is a very popular stop for visitors today, many of whom still have trouble separating fact from fiction. Call 800-989-7800 for more information and directions.

The Kennedy Legacy. On November 23, 1963, President John F. Kennedy was shot and killed near Daley Plaza in downtown Dallas. Against the advice of some of his closest advisors, Kennedy chose to make the trip in hopes of bolstering his sagging political fortunes. The many theories surrounding the assassination are enough to keep you reading for a lifetime. Lo-

Huge lakes surrounded by piney woods are liberally sprinkled throughout east Texas.

cated on Elm Street, a small museum on the sixth floor of the **Texas School Book Depository** (214-747-6660; www.jkf.org) outlines the life, death, and legacy of JFK. You are even able to look out the window from which **Lee Oswald** made his shots. Take a stroll over to the infamous "grassy knoll" and draw your own conclusions. An auto tour using the same type of limousine in which JFK was riding passes the spot where he was killed and plays recordings of radio reports from that day as it covers the ground to the hospital.

    Texas Cowboy Hall of Fame. Located in an old horse and mule barn at 128 E. Exchange Avenue in the Fort Worth Stockyards National Historical District, the Cowboy Hall of Fame celebrates the life and times of Texas cowboys who have excelled in the sports of rodeo and cutting. Twenty-seven individuals are honored with displays of photos, memorabilia, and audio-visual presentations concerning their exploits and accomplishments. A special section of the museum gives tribute to the famous boot maker, **John Justin.** Although he arrived in Dallas virtually penniless, he became a multi-millionaire through hard work and determination, building the largest boot factory in the world. Later, Justin generously gave back to his beloved Dallas, both in monetary donations and through serving in many civic capacities.

The antique wagon display may seem a little out of step with the rest of this facility, but it is an interesting visit nonetheless. The more than sixty wagons on display, including a Sicilian cart from the 1750s with intricate iron work and painted scenes, and a Welsh funeral hearse complete with beveled glass windows, gold leaf paint, and plumes. For more information, visit their website (www.texascowboyhalloffame.com) or call them at 817-626-7131.

Texas Cowgirl Hall of Fame. This museum is the only one in the world dedicated to honoring and documenting the lives of women who have distinguished themselves while exemplifying the pioneer spirit of the American West. The current 159 honorees not only include cowgirls and ranch women, but also writers, artists, and teachers who made their mark on the settling of the west. Honorees include **Narcissa Prentiss Whitman** (the first woman to cross the Rockies), as well as the renowned artist **Georgia O'Keefe**. Located at 1720 Gendy Street (817-336-4475; www.cowgirl.net).

Fort Worth Stockyards and National Historic District. The complex, located at the site of the original stockyards at 131 E. Exchange Avenue, includes some of the original pens. Although it is an active cattle exchange, most of the trading is done via satellite today. You are welcome to sit in on one of the auctions, but be careful about moving your hands and feet or you might end up going home with a steer!

As the stockyards declined and development crept into the area, the U.S. Department of Interior made the entire complex into a National Historical District in 1976, to prevent future "improvements." Today, it's home to nearly 50 livestock commission companies, in addition to numerous other offices (mostly attorneys and architects). The district is dotted with saloons, restaurants, western wear stores, and just about anything you can think of pertaining to the cowboy and his life.

The **Fort Worth Visitor Center** (817-625-5087), across the street from the Exchange building, can supply you with a wealth of brochures and maps to get you on your way. They even offer walking tours of the entire complex several times a day.

Day 27   Dallas to Crockett

Distance *230 miles*

Features *The good stuff will begin after a stretch of high-speed riding over open prairie to get out of Dallas. Consider a stop in Tyler, the Rose Capitol of America, and a visit to oldest Spanish mission in east Texas, reconstructed on its original site.*

From the intersection of Loop 635 and I-20 on the east side of Dallas, take I-20 east for 89 miles; take Exit 556 onto Hwy. 69 and head south, toward the city of Tyler. After 9 miles, you will intersect with Loop 323 on the outskirts of Tyler. Turn right and follow Loop 323 for two miles to the intersection with Hwy. 31 (Front Street). If you care to visit the Municipal Rose Garden, Visitors' Center and Museum (see below), turn left here and just follow the signs for a few short blocks. If you do not wish to make this stop, turn right here.

Lumbering is big business in East Texas. Keep an eye out for debris left on the road. (photo by TxDOT)

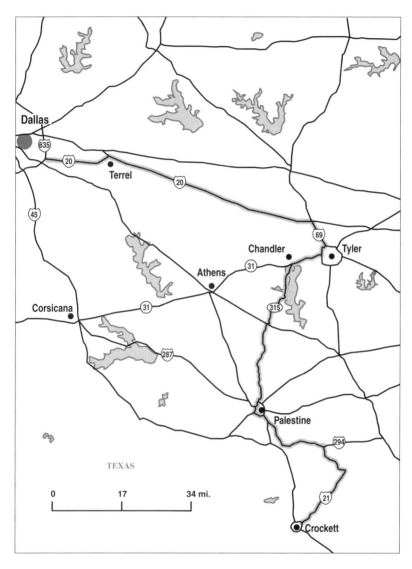

The city of **Tyler,** with a population of more than 80,000 is by far the largest city in northeast Texas. It is called **the Rose Capitol of America,** and rightly so, as it provides more than 20 percent of the rose bushes sold in the country. Growing, displaying, and selling roses is the number one industry here. This industry supports the local tourist business with thousands of people descending on the city for the famous **Tyler Rose Festival** held during mid-October each year.

A visit to this restored, failed Spanish mission in east Texas can give real insight to the struggle for land rights between the original French and Spanish settlers.

✪ *Side Trip*

Roses are in bloom May through October, and are proudly on display at the **Tyler Municipal Rose Garden** located at 420 S. Rose Park Drive. Covering more than 14 acres, the garden contains over 30,000 bushes of seemingly endless varieties. Adjoining the garden is the **Tyler Rose Garden Center and Museum.** If you have the slightest interest in flowers in general, and roses in particular, this can make for a wonderful stop, even when the plants are not in bloom. After your visit, retrace your route and continue west on Hwy. 31.

Follow Hwy. 31 for 7 miles and turn left onto Hwy. 315 in the town of Chambers. While Hwy. 31 is a major highway, the views of all the lakes and woodlands beside the road make it quite worthwhile. After turning onto

Hwy. 315, get ready for 41 miles of absolutely wonderful motorcycle riding, as few roads this good exist in the world. The road is typically in good shape, so if you want to take the rpm's up, enjoy. At slower speeds you'll have time to wish it all would never end. This may be the best motorcycle road in all of east Texas.

Turn right onto Hwy. 155, and a very short distance later, turn left onto Loop 256 to stay on the outskirts of Palestine. After 5 miles, turn left onto Hwy. 287. Another 5 miles later, turn left onto Hwy. 2419, proceed 11 miles, and turn left onto Hwy. 294.

After departing **Palestine,** the roads become smaller again with the limbs of the trees often draping over the entire roadway. After 15 miles on Hwy. 294, turn right onto Hwy. 228. Three miles later, turn left onto Hwy. 3016; in another 5 miles or so, turn right onto Hwy. 227. Four miles later, turn right onto Hwy. 21.

○ *Side Trip*

At the Hwy. 21 intersection, turn left and 1-1/2 miles later the **Mission Tejas State Historical Park** will be on your left. This is the location of the first Spanish mission built in east Texas to aid their efforts of stopping the intrusion of the French. Originally established in 1690, it has a colorful history of abandonments, destructions, and reconstructions over the years. It was finally relocated in 1730. A replica of the mission was built in the 1930s and is open to the public today. The setting is one of rustic beauty and tranquility common to the east Texas piney woods. If you are camping, sites are available with water and showers. It makes a great site on which to end the day.

After visiting the park, retrace your route and pick up Hwy. 227, which runs concurrently with Hwy. 21 for about a half-mile before veering off to the left. Take this turn. This is a delicious motorcycle road for the next 13 miles. Turn right onto Hwy. 7, proceed 21 miles, and turn left onto Loop 304 in the small town of Crockett. The **Crockett Inn,** located at 1600 Loop 304 east ($60; 409-544-5611) will be on your right just down the road. This motel, while somewhat overpriced, is really the only decent place to stay in the area. It does have an excellent restaurant with fresh homemade bread.

Day 28   Crockett to College Station

Distance *210 miles*

Features *This day offers more opportunities to ride the east Texas woodlands and enjoy this countryside so close to Houston. You can also visit the Texas State Prison in Huntsville and see the "World's Largest Statue to an American Hero." Some of these roads today will be as good or better than you have ever ridden.*

From the Crockett Inn, retrace yesterday's path on Loop 310 and turn right onto Hwy. 7. After 16 miles, continue through the small town of Kennard, and about a half-mile past the yellow blinking light, proceed straight ahead onto Hwy. 357.

After 11 miles, go straight ahead and pick up Hwy. 233. Another 5 miles down the road, turn right onto Hwy. 358. Thirteen miles later, turn left onto

At 65 feet in height, this statue of Sam Houston just outside Huntsville is truly "larger than life."

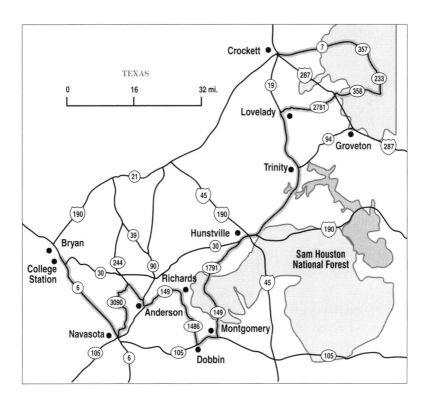

Hwy. 2781 in the town of Pennington. Follow this road for 7 miles and turn right onto Hwy. 1280.

In another 8 miles, turn left onto Hwy. 19. You will have been riding the backroads of the **Davy Crockett National Forest** all morning. While the roads are not very dramatic through here, they are a nice, traffic-free rides through the country and woods. The next 34 miles on Hwy. 19 will be more open and prone to higher speed. Turn right onto Hwy. 30 and you'll enter the town of Huntsville.

The city of **Huntsville,** with a population that exceeds 20,000, is most famous as the home of the **Texas Department of Criminal Justice.** With seven prisons that can house up to 13,690 inmates at any given time, this is Huntsville's most important industry. The department employs nearly 7,000 people.

Texas justice is harsh. The state more often than not leads all states in the number of executions each year (Florida is usually second, but did beat out Texas *one year).* In 1997, there were 37 executions here. In total, nearly 600 people have lost their lives at the hands of the state in Huntsville.

To get a look at the original prison, built in 1849, turn left onto Avenue I; as you enter town on 11th Street, you can circumnavigate the complex. There is even a **Texas Prison Museum** at 1113 12th Street, that includes taped interviews of people who have since been executed; the original electric chair, **"Old Sparky;"** various items confiscated from prisoners over the years; Bonnie and Clyde's rifles; and more. You can even "visit" a 9 x 6 cell.

After returning to 11th Street, turn left, continue to the county courthouse, and turn left onto Sam Houston Avenue. **Charlotte's Ribs & Thangs** located at 2530 Sycamore and Sam Houston Avenue offers some of the best Bar-B-Q available anywhere. Approximately 5 miles down this road, you'll spot the "typically Texas" **World's Largest Statue to an American Hero** on your left. Of course, it honors Sam Houston.

If you reach the interstate, you have gone too far. To best view the 67-foot statue, park your bike at the visitors' center and take a short stroll down the pleasant wooded path. There is plenty of information in the visitors' center about Huntsville and the prisons, including a suggested driving tour of the city and the system.

Leaving the visitors' center, continue west on Hwy. 30 for about 5 miles, then turn left onto Hwy. 1791. Follow this pleasing road for 17 miles and then turn left onto Hwy. 149. The speed limit on Hwy. 149 is 55 mph; if you ride the speed limit, this will be one of the most enjoyable touring rides of your life. If you care to ride this road at 70 mph, you have a super sport-bike road.

After about 12 miles, turn right onto Hwy. 105 in Montgomery. After 5 more miles, take another right onto Hwy. 1486. Fourteen miles later, turn left onto Hwy. 2819 toward Anderson. Just before getting to Anderson, there is a fork in this road without any other indications; take the right-hand fork toward Anderson.

Ten miles after getting onto Hwy. 2819, turn right onto Hwy. 90, proceed a mere 2 miles, and turn left onto Hwy. 244. Six miles later, turn left onto Hwy. 3090. For the next 10 miles you can ride this delightful road at as high a speed as you want, but be alert, as it contains some serious curves that can sneak up on you.

After 10 miles, follow Hwy. 3090 off to the right, proceed another 6 miles, and turn right onto Hwy. 6—a high-speed, four-lane road that is not, however, an interstate. Stay on the lookout for crossing and entering traffic. After 19 miles, exit left onto Hwy. 6 Business. As you enter **College Station,** home of **Texas A&M University,** you will see signs welcoming you to "Aggieland."

➡ The Raven - Sam Houston

The first president of the Republic of Texas, Sam Houston was the earliest in a long line of colorful, controversial, and illustrious Texas politicians. Born in Virginia in 1793, his family soon moved to Tennessee. As a youth, he ran away from home because he didn't like to work or go to school and lived with the Cherokee Indians for more than three years. These Indians called him The Raven, and the name stayed with him for the rest of his life.

Tiring of the Indian lifestyle, Houston returned to civilization and read for the law. He joined the army and soon became a protégé of Andrew Jackson. After practicing law for a while, he soon found his true calling in politics, serving as governor of Tennessee. Houston served three terms to the U.S. House of Representatives before returning to live with the Indians.

In 1832 Sam Houston moved to Texas for unknown reasons, possibly for land speculation, maybe as a U.S. agent to urge entrance into the Union, or, perhaps, to help establish an independent nation. Whatever his original intentions, he soon became a major figure in the Texas fight for independence and subsequent operations of the new nation.

Houston was a signer of the Texas Declaration of Independence and was named as commander-in-chief of the Armies of Texas during that fight. He led his men to victory over Santa Anna at San Jacinto and was soon elected president of the Republic.

Because of Houston's size and reputation as a heavy drinker, he was called the Big Drunk. He was re-elected president in 1841. After Texas joined the Union, Houston served as a U.S. senator and later, as governor of the state. His career was doomed, however, by strong stands in favor of Indian rights and his pre-Civil War opposition to succession from the Union. His third wife, a highly religious Baptist woman, influenced him to quit his heavy drinking and move to Huntsville as a private citizen, where he died.

It's hard to determine what is fact or fiction among the many stories that circulate about this man. That he was a natural-born leader, had amazing abilities to govern despite his personal problems, and is a true hero in the hearts and minds of the people of Texas is about all of which we can be sure.   ★

There are almost unlimited places to stay and eat along this road. A good, basic place to stay on the edge of the campus is the **E-Z Travel Motor Inn** ($50; 409-693-5822) at 2007 Texas Avenue S. (Hwy. 6 Business) with a good steak house and Bar-B-Q place next door. Several other dining options are within walking distance. As this is a university town, your choice of watering holes is almost boundless.

➡ The University of Texas vs. Texas A&M

The state of Texas contains many fine universities. The two largest, each with several campuses throughout the state, have student populations approaching 100,000. Both the main campuses, University of Texas at Austin and Texas A&M at College Station, boast student populations of about 50,000. These two world-class schools have received awards for academic excellence, and graduates from each usually go on to successful careers in many fields.

These two schools project different cultures and each is fiercely proud of its own. The University of Texas is considered the more sophisticated of the two. Students and alumni are often referred to as "Tea Sippers" as a reflection of their social graces. Texas A&M was originally founded as an agricultural college and their loyalists are called "Aggies." A line in one of the schools fight songs further enhances this image, "Fight, Farmers, Fight." As with any generalization, these images no longer hold true to form on either campus.

Students and alumni from the two schools co-exist peacefully during most of the year, working side by side, doing business together, attending the same churches, and sharing the same neighborhoods. However, it is still considered somewhat of a social blunder to seat graduates from the two schools side-by-side at a formal dinner or reception.

The armistice comes to a halt each year around Thanksgiving, when the two football teams face off on the gridiron. No matter the record of either team, the pride and honor of each school is on the line. It reminds one of the Civil War, in that it pits brother against brother, husband against wife. Business partners take their respective sides and friends quit talking to one another the week building up to the battle. Taunts are hurled, practical jokes abound, and bets are placed not so much to reflect the actual expected outcome of the game, but purely as a matter of honor. The game itself reminds one of war, as both teams rise to the occasion and give it their all.

A few days after the game, things begin to return to normal until the next year. As a visitor to Texas, enjoy the hullabaloo. To stay out of the fray, it is best to keep your mouth shut, as fans of neither school will believe anyone could be neutral on such an important issue.   ★

Actually there are two towns, College Station and **Bryan.** If it weren't for the city limit signs, however, you wouldn't know the difference. The permanent population is estimated to be something like 50,000. But don't let this mislead you. The 50,000 students of Texas A&M University swell the local ranks each year.

The university is the overriding driving force in the economy and the social life of the cities. The Texas A&M campus covers more than 5,000 acres and a more loyal and fervent student body, alumni, staff, and followers will not be found anywhere on the planet. Originally established in 1871 as an agricultural and mechanical college (hence the nickname "Aggies"), it was originally an all-male school with required military training until 1964—the year the first women ("Maggies") were admitted. Military training then became optional.

Today the "Corps" has an enrollment exceeding 2,000 and they make quite a sight in football game parades. Today, the world-class university contains 10 colleges covering all courses of study. The **George H. Bush Presidential Library and Museum,** located on campus, details the life and accomplishments of this former president, and is an oft-visited site by outsiders, as well.

➡ Texas Justice

Texas history is steeped with outlaws, savages, and invaders that have always been met with swift and harsh justice. The Texas Rangers were known for their ruthlessness in handling Indians, Mexicans, and outlaws. The U.S. Army protected much of Texas for a time and handled offenders as do most armies: the suspected lawbreakers were rarely tried.

After the Civil War, carpetbaggers from the northern states poured into Texas to line their pockets at the expense of the general population. Groups of ordinary citizens, called Regulators, took it upon themselves to bring order and punish criminals. These vigilantes held sway for several years until decent state law enforcement was re-established. In Goliad, the "hanging tree" on the town square says all that needs to be said about their methods.

Today, justice in Texas follows the rest of the nation in adhering to constitutional rights, and the legal system is consistent with other states. However, Texas Rangers still have a reputation for being rough and tough when faced with apprehending criminals. They also enjoy the well-earned reputation of being some of the best in the business.

When faced with today's Texas judges and juries, a criminal learns firsthand the general attitude of the public regarding punishment. Prison sentences are most often set to the maximum possible and the "hanging tree" is still used frequently (although now it is a lethal injection). Since the death penalty was reinstated, Texas leads the nation by far in its number of executions. If you plan to break the law, choose a different state. ★

Day 29   College Station to Galveston

Distance *235 miles*

Features *This day starts off on flatish rural roads alongside farms and pastures, but a few curves and sweepers can make for some fun. You'll loop around the megalopolis of Houston and then take a backroad route to some of the most hallowed ground in the state of Texas, see a large inland lake containing one of the world's largest collection of yachts, and visit the NASA headquarters.*

From your motel, go to the intersection of Hwy. 6 Business and Hwy. 60 on the north side of the campus. Turn left onto Hwy. 60, a four-lane ride for 14 miles. Turn left onto Hwy. 2155. By now, you will have left the city and are once again on nice country motorcycle roads.

Follow Hwy. 2155 for 6 miles, then turn left onto Hwy. 1361. If you wish to see a small farming town typical of this area, take a right on Spur 2155 as you approach Snook; in a few short blocks it will take you back to Hwy. 2155, where you'll turn right.

Wildlife refuges along the Texas gulf coast are famous for their birds. (photo by Randy Green/TxDOT)

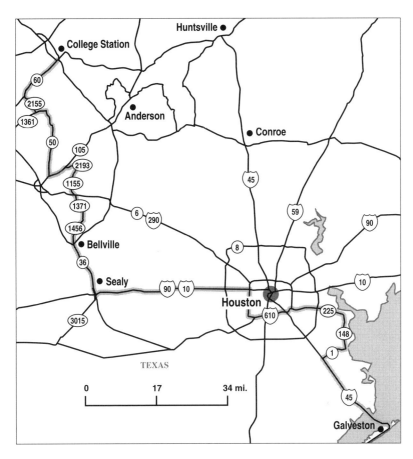

After 3 miles on Hwy. 1361, turn right onto Hwy. 50, a main highway that nonetheless makes for a very enjoyable ride through pasturelands and farms. Nineteen miles later, turn left onto Hwy. 105, a major four-laner, but you will only be on it for 6 miles. Turn right onto Hwy. 2193. The next 27 miles of riding will be your last chance on this route to enjoy rural roads, so slow down and enjoy them.

After 3 miles on Hwy. 2193, turn right on Hwy. 1155 and 8 miles later, at the T-intersection, turn left onto Hwy. 1371. At the STOP sign, go right onto Hwy. 1371, proceed 7 miles, and turn right onto Hwy. 1456 toward Bellville. After 9 miles take a left onto Hwy. 36; in about 15 miles you will intersect with I-10 east, only 45 miles from the intersection with Loop 610 in Houston. The ride into Houston will give you a good idea as to just how large this city really is. Development extends over 20 miles before you reach the "outer" loop.

The more than 1,000 restored Victorian mansions in Galveston are enough to attract many visitors. (photo by Richard Reynolds/TxDOT)

✪ *Alternate Route*

If you have it, consider spending some of your extra time on this next section, and taking longer than the routing recommends. If you have to keep it moving, and can't take the time to see the sights this time around, you could go directly to the intersection of I-45 south from Loop 610. I-45 south will take you directly to Galveston from there.

Turn south on Loop 610 and follow it around town to the intersection with Hwy. 225 east.

The next stretch of road has so many things to see and do that I have featured it in Day 21 as well. For even more detail on what follows, or for information for continuing on to Houston, please refer to that section of the book.

Traffic on the freeway system in and around Houston is usually heavy. Hang in there and stay alert as you navigate your way out of town. You will soon go through the towns of Pasadena and Deer Park. Most people are overwhelmed the first time through here by the sights and smells of the massive **crude oil refineries** and **petrochemical plants** that line this road.

After 11 miles, exit onto Battleground Road (Hwy. 134) and follow signs to the San Jacinto Monument, a pilgrimage Texans take quite seriously. Just 2-1/2 miles up the road, turn right to the battleground and monument.

The **San Jacinto Historical Complex** is located on the site where the Texicans defeated **General Santa Anna** and his army to secure their independence from Mexico. Leaving the battleground, follow the signs directing you to the permanent mooring of the **battleship Texas,** the last surviving battleship to serve in both World War I and World War II. It has been extensively renovated and is open for tours. From the battleship you can get a close look at the huge tankers carrying crude oil, petroleum products, and petrochemicals in and out of the ship channel.

After your visit to the San Jacinto Complex, retrace your route on Hwy. 134 to the intersection with Hwy. 225 and turn left. After 4 miles, turn right (south) onto 146. From this point, you will still be in an urban area, but the traffic thins to some extent and you can give your nerves a rest. After 9 miles you'll need to take a right onto NASA Road 1 in **Clear Lake,** a wonderful sheltered cove for yachts and boats of every description, with access to the Gulf of Mexico via **Galveston Bay.**

Luxury resorts and world-class accommodations are in plentiful supply in Galveston. Just bring money.

Six miles along NASA Road 1, you'll see the **Lyndon B. Johnson Space Center** on your right, mission control for all NASA space operations. To see the facility, you must first visit **Space Center Houston,** located on your right about a block past the NASA entranceway. Interesting exhibits and films outline the U.S. space program, and some of the original spacecraft are on display. Trams to the NASA facility itself operate on an almost continuous basis. You could spend a whole day here.

The quickest and easiest way to reach your destination of Galveston Island is to continue on NASA 1 until the intersection with I-45. From there, head south for approximately 28 miles until you cross the bridge onto the island. As you travel along this road, the traffic thins, and you will soon be in a rural area of vast marshlands. After crossing onto the island, the road becomes Broadway (Avenue J); continue straight ahead until you reach the ocean.

After passing though some fairly seedy neighborhoods, you'll be approaching the ocean, and Galveston's restored Victorian homes will brighten your outlook. When you can see the ocean, turn right, to put yourself on Seawall Blvd. (for some reason, this intersection is marked as 6th Street).

This seawall was constructed after a hurricane in 1900 wiped out Galveston. The city never regained its former prominence as the major city in Texas.

There is a good selection of motels and hotels in Galveston in every price range. A good medium-priced place to stay is **Gaido's Seaside Inn** located at 3828 Seawall Blvd. ($60; 409-762-9626, 800-525-0064). As everywhere, a room with an ocean view commands a premium; you can save about $10 if you don't mind a view of a parking lot. Note also that the fenced, locked parking area for these rooms is quieter and more secure than the one facing the seawall.

Gaido's restaurant, next to the inn, is deemed by many to be the best place to eat on the island. **Casey's Seafood Restaurant,** located in the motel, has the same fare at a much lower price, as it has the same owners and operators as Gaido's.

The nearest camping to the city of Galveston is about 6 miles southwest off Seawall Blvd., on 61st S.E. at **Galveston Island State Park** ($15; 409-737-1222). This is a beautiful setting with nature trails that go from the ocean on one side to the bay on the other. Galveston State Park accepts reservations and the facilities include flush toilets, showers, grills, and picnic tables.

Check the **Galveston Convention and Visitors Bureau** at 2106 Seawall if you are interested in touring the many Victorian. For $1, a trolley will take you through **The Strand** and **Silk Stocking,** two of the historic districts.

To get an idea of how the rich of Galveston lived during its heyday, visit **The Grand,** the opera house built in 1894. Located at 2020 Post Office, it is a magnificent building. Self-guided tours are available of the interior. It is true opulence.

The **Bishop's Palace,** located at 1402 Broadway, will be on your left as you enter Galveston. The **American Institute of Architecture** has designated this Victorian structure as the second most impressive in the United States. Original in every detail and carefully preserved, tours are offered daily. If you plan to see only one of these homes, this should be it.

For more of Galveston's history, see Day 21.

Day 30   Galveston to Jasper

Distance *205 miles*

Features *This day offers a nice mix of riding. Starting out on the ocean, a nice ferry ride brings you to flat marshlands with a Cajun flavor. In Beaumont, you can visit Spindletop and an interesting Harley-Davidson dealership with its next-door H.O.G.G. House. Sweepers and low hills surrounded by heavy woods and bayous bring the day to an end in a fisherman's mecca.*

Return back east on Seawall Blvd. and turn right onto Hwy. 87 (at the intersection where you turned right yesterday to get onto Seawall). In just a block or two, turn left at the sign indicating the ferry landing.

As you approach the loading area, you more than likely will see a long line of vehicles waiting their turn to load. As is the rule at most all ferries, motorcycles can go to the front, as they can load in spaces autos cannot. Ignore the signs about no passing or cutting in and continue to the front of the line. Unfortunately, some motorists do not understand or appreciate this practice, and you may be subjected to some horn honking and hand gestures. However, be assured you are doing what is correct and expected.

The **Boliver Ferry** is free and takes about 15 minutes to make its transit, time well spent watching for marine life and gazing at the array of ocean going ships passing by or at anchor waiting for dock space.

Almost immediately after leaving the ferry you will notice that you are in an entirely different culture. In this flat marshland, people speak with a Cajun accent, eating places go from offering Bar-B-Q and chicken-fried steak to specializing in crawfish etouffee, shrimp gumbo, smoked boudain and other Cajun delicacies. After debarking, continue on Hwy. 87 for 28 miles and then turn left onto Hwy. 124.

✪ *Alternate Route*

At the time this book was written, Hwy. 87 was closed past Hwy. 24 due to hurricane damage. My efforts to obtain estimates as to when, or even if, it will be repaired received mixed, confusing, and unreliable results. The following directions assume this highway will remain closed and routes you on to Port Arthur another way.

If you find that Hwy. 87 has been reopened, I suggest you take it.

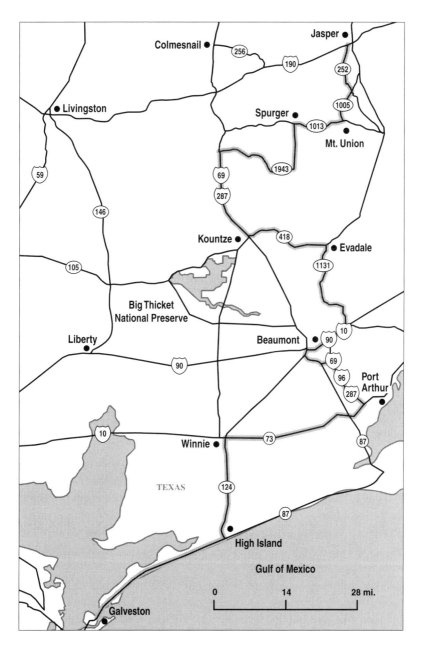

Continue on Hwy. 124 for 21 miles and turn right onto Hwy. 73 in Winnie. Between the ferry and Winnie, the route is mostly flat and straight, through marshlands, though you will have an occasional view of the ocean and bay. For an interesting rest stop, check out one of the many **bird sanctu-**

aries along the way. One of the most pleasant, a place called **High Island,** is located on your left shortly after getting on Hwy. 124. Although this spot is less than 100 feet high, it was used as a refuge by early settlers during hurricanes.

As you approach **Winnie** and gain some elevation, you'll be riding through large rice fields. Winnie is the self-proclaimed **Rice Capitol of Texas.** On Hwy. 73, expect 30 miles of four-lane, high-speed road to the left-hand onto Hwy, 69 in Port Arthur.

Fourteen miles on Hwy. 69 will have you in Beaumont. Take the Highland Avenue Exit and the **Spindletop/Gladys City Boomtown** and **Lucas Gusher Monument** will be on your right. You can explore a reproduction of the boomtown that grew up near the site of the first Spindletop well. A fifty-eight foot, pink granite monument commemorates the well alongside recreated examples of the original wooden drilling rigs. Several of the buildings in town are furnished in the era.

After your visit, turn left out of the parking lot, go one block and turn right, go to the first traffic light and turn right. This will bring you back to Hwy. 69, where you should turn right. Continue on Hwy. 69 for 4 miles to the intersection with I-10. Take I-10 east to the first exit (College), go under the freeway, and turn left onto the frontage road. It will be impossible to miss the huge Harley-Davidson sign.

Cowboy Harley-Davidson (409-839-4464; www.cowboyharley.com) and the adjoining H.O.G.G. House are sights not to be missed! This dealership looks out of place in Beaumont, Texas. You might expect something like it in Beverly Hills or Palm Beach. With more than 50,000 feet of display area housing over 200 motorcycles and all accessories known to man, the inside of the building matches the magnificence of the exterior.

The **H.O.G.G. House** next door was built by the dealership and is home for the local Harley Owners Group, which has more than 300 current members. It has a very upscale interior and all the comforts of home. Even if you are not a Harley fan, it's worth a stop, and everyone is welcome at the clubhouse.

After your visit, get back on I-10 east for 10 miles and take Exit 861A in Vidor. Go under the freeway and head north on Hwy. 105. Continue on Hwy. 105 for 4 miles and turn left onto Hwy. 1131. This 15 miles of road will be an introduction to the woods of east Texas, full of sweepers and curves alongside thick forests. Enjoy.

Turn left onto Hwy. 105, go one mile, and turn left onto Hwy. 96 toward Silsbee. After 5 miles on Hwy. 96, exit onto Hwy. 96 Business/418. Follow the frontage road to the T-intersection and turn right, following the signs to

The massive swamps and bayous found in East Texas are a surprise to many a rider. (photo by Stan A. Williams/TxDOT)

Hwy. 418. After only a half-mile, turn left onto Hwy. 418, a nice little road that meanders through the forest with gentle sweepers. After 11 miles, turn right onto Hwy. 69, a major four-laner that makes up for its lack of challenge in beautiful views. Seven miles later, turn right at the signs indicating the **Big Thicket Visitors' Center,** which will be on your left almost immediately after making this turn.

The area that makes up the **Big Thicket National Preserve** was, until after the Civil War, a vast, thick forest containing many rivers, bayous, and sloughs. Neither the native Indians nor the white man had attempted to penetrate or settle it. It did, however, serve as a haven for draft dodgers, outlaws, and runaway slaves, as they could literally "get lost" in its more than 5,000 square miles.

After the war, the lumber industry started to harvest the massive amount of timber in the Big Thicket. In 1974 it was made into a national preserve to protect what remained of this natural wonder; today it includes more than 100,000 acres. The Big Thicket has been called "America's Ark" and the United Nations has placed it on its list of **International Biosphere Reserves Worth Protecting.** It has diverse flora and fauna not found anywhere else in the United States.

The helpful staff at Big Thicket Visitors' Center have some excellent brochures outlining the scientific aspect of the park, even if most people are content with just gawking at the woodlands. If you are on a dual-sport bike, pick up the excellent map of delightful dirt roads in the area. A brochure outlining a half-day auto tour tells you of sights along the loop and is also applicable for those on street bikes.

Primitive camping is allowed in the preserve, but a free permit must be obtained at the visitors' center first. Because areas around the preserve are still being harvested, be on the lookout for the many log-carrying trucks you will be encountering. They leave a lot of loose bark and other debris in their wake. Make sure your face shield is down when meeting or approaching one.

Leaving the visitors' center, return to Hwy. 69, and turn right. After 4 miles, you'll have to decide whether to continue on pavement or face a little bit of dirt. If dirt, take a right turn onto Hwy. 3063 (this is by far the more interesting route). When I was last through here, the roads were in good shape and could be ridden comfortably on a street bike. After about 3 miles, turn left onto Hicksbaugh Road, and three miles later turn right onto W. Midway Road. The dirt section ends 8 miles further on, when you turn right onto Hwy. 1943. At the T-intersection with Hwy. 92, turn left and follow the rest of the route from there. This ride through the heart of the **Turkey Creek Unit** of the Big Thicket is wonderful and I recommend it highly.

❂ *Alternate Route*

If you do not wish to ride dirt, just continue 4 miles on Hwy. 69 to the town of Warren, and then turn right onto Hwy. 1943, a very pleasant motorcycle ride through the woods. In 16 miles, turn left onto Hwy. 92.

Suitable lodging is hard to find in the small towns around here. I recommend you continue on to Jasper: following 92 north for 8 miles, turn right onto Hwy. 1013 in the town of Spurger, proceed 10 miles, and then turn left onto Hwy. 1005. After 10 more miles, turn left onto Hwy. 252 toward Jasper. After 7 miles, turn right onto Hwy. 190 into Jasper.

The **Best Western Motel** at 205 W. Gibson ($50; 409-344-7767) is a more than adequate place to stay. It will be on your right as you enter town. Next to the motel, **Elijah's Café,** serves up heaping plates of down-home Southern cooking. There are several cheaper independent motels in town, but I don't recommend them.

If you prefer a more rural setting and are not on a tight budget, turn left onto Hwy. 190 and less than a mile later, turn right onto Hwy. 63. After 8 miles, turn right onto Hwy. 255, proceed another 5 miles, and turn left onto

Hwy. 1007. You will be three-quarters of a mile from the reception area for **Rayburn Country Resort** ($55; 800-882-1442, 409-698-2444), complete with a 27-hole golf course, is located on **Lake Sam Rayburn** and sits on a 3,000-acre patch of piney woods. Although the price for your room is not much more than downtown, the food, while good, is expensive. Expect a tab for dinner to approach $20.

If you are camping, turn left when you intersect with Hwy. 190, go 12 miles, and then turn right onto Park Road 48 to **Martin Dies, Jr. State Park,** truly wonderful setting on the banks of Lake Sam Rayburn. There are some screened shelters available and all campsites have water. For reservations, phone 512-389-8900.

Jasper, a town of approximately 9,000 people, is self-proclaimed as the **"Jewel of the Forest."** While the town was founded in 1860, it was completely destroyed by a fire in 1901. Jasper was rebuilt almost entirely of brick buildings, and you can stroll the downtown district in a short time. The people here are very proud of their town and make great efforts to make visitors feel welcome.

Outdoor activities attract most visitors to Jasper: camping, hiking, observing nature, and enjoying the wonderful lakes nearby. Fishing is big sport, and several professional bass tournaments are held here every year. The motels go so far as to designate parking places to accommodate a pickup truck with attached 20-foot bass boat.

Day 31   Jasper to Jefferson or Shreveport

Distance   *To Jefferson: 175 miles; to Shreveport: 195 miles*

Features   *This superb day of riding on some very good roads with many opportunities to stop and take in the natural sights. As a final destination, you'll have two very different choices: Shreveport, for a night of bright lights and gambling, or Jefferson, a sleepy old restored Southern town that will make you think you are in the bayous of the coast during the 1870s.*

Leave Jasper on Hwy. 190 west. The next 20 miles of high-speed road is a visual delight, especially in the spring when wildflowers line the sides of the roads. The many lakes and bayous containing giant cypress trees draped with Spanish moss run contrary to most folks image of Texas. After this run, turn right onto Hwy. 256, every rider's dream road running through the forest with gentle hills and numerous sweepers. Very fast riding is not safe, as your line of sight is limited by the heavy vegetation and healthy deer population.

After 13 miles, turn right onto Hwy. 69, go only 2 miles, and make another right turn onto Hwy. 255. For the next 19 miles, you can pick up your speed, as the sides of the highway have been cleared back a good distance and you can see through the curves. Turn left onto Hwy. 1007, proceed 5 miles, and turn left onto Hwy. 96.

For the last few miles, you will have had some excellent views of **Lake Sam Rayburn,** the largest lake in Texas, covering more than 114,000 acres. It is thoroughly enjoyed by fishermen and utilized for all water sports, which can add a lot of interest to your rest stops. As the road goes on, it passes the dam that creates this lake—truly an engineering marvel.

Eleven miles up Hwy. 96, turn right turn onto Hwy. 83, and follow signs as the road works its way through the small town of Hemphill. You may have noticed by now that the further north you get in east Texas, the more frequent and pronounced the hills become. Five miles out of Hemphill, turn left onto Hwy. 3121, go another 5 miles, and turn left onto Hwy. 21. Five miles later, turn right onto Hwy. 87, a major road that is, nevertheless, a delight to ride. Although you are now going through the **Sabine National Forest,** some of the land along the road has been developed to pasture. After 16 miles, turn right onto Hwy. 139.

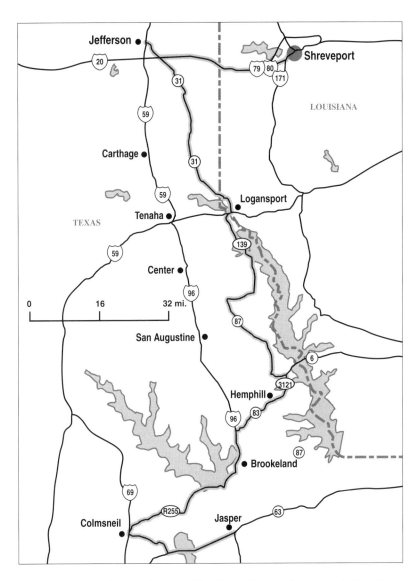

Slow down and enjoy the next 25 miles on Hwy. 139, as this is just about as good as it gets, with lots of hills, curves, and beautiful views. Turn right onto Hwy. 84 and cross the **Sabine River** into Louisiana at Logansport. Almost immediately after crossing the river, turn left onto Hwy. 169, proceed 3 miles, and then turn left onto Hwy. 31, which will take you back into Texas. Follow Hwy. 31 for 38 miles to the intersection with I-20—a pleasant ride with the potential for a good speed.

The massive swamps and bayous found in East Texas are excellent for bass fishing. (photo by John Suhrstedt/TxDOT)

○ *Option*

When you reach I-20 you must pick your destination for the evening. If you would like to try your hand at some riverboat gambling, head east to Shreveport. If you prefer a small quiet old Southern town with an interesting historic district, take I-20 west.

If you're headed to **Shreveport,** just follow I-20 east for 39 miles. According to Louisiana law, all casinos must be on riverboats. It didn't take operators long to put the casinos themselves on permanent barges moored to the riverbank and build huge hotel complexes and support facilities on the adjoining bank. The two buildings are connected by covered "boarding walkways." In fact, you are given a "boarding pass" as you enter the casinos.

Almost all major gambling operators are represented off Exit 20, offering everything you would expect to find in Las Vegas. In addition to any losses your visit might incur, consider that the cost of the room will be around $100. Dining opportunities abound. I like the **Isle of Capri Casino** because it has nickel slots on the third floor. If you want to gamble, but would rather not spend so much on a room, continue to Exit 21 and check out the **Motel 6** ($30). The cab ride back to the casino will only be a buck or two.

If you're headed to **Jefferson,** take I-20 west for only a mile or two, exit onto Hwy. 59 north, and go about 19 miles. As you enter the city, turn right onto Taylor to get into the historic section of the city.

For a city its size, Jefferson has an amazing array of places to stay. It you prefer a standard motel unit, try the **Inn of Jefferson,** located on your right as you come into town, at 400 S. Wolcott ($45; 903-665-3983), a new motel within walking distance of the historic district. The **Excelsior House** at 211 W. Austin has been in continuous operation since the 1850s ($85+; 903-665-2513) at the center of things, and the interior has been faithfully restored and furnished in the period. To narrow down the long list of historic B&Bs in the area, contact Jefferson Reservation Service (887-603-2535; www.jeffersonreservationservice.com). Try the fresh seafood, Cajun and Creole dishes at the **Black Swan** on 210 Austin. The helpings are abundant and the price is moderate.

There are no camping facilities in Jefferson proper. Fortunately, there are plenty nearby that are excellent. Try **Johnson Creek Park** located on **Lake o' The Pines,** which is operated by the Corps of Engineers (903-755-2435). There are 22 campsites sitting in a beautiful rural setting in the pines beside the lake. Facilities include flush toilets, showers, and grills. To get there, take Hwy. 49 west out of town, turn left onto Hwy. 729 for 15 miles, and go south on the park road for one mile.

Located on **Big Cypress Bayou,** the town of Jefferson was once a major river port that boasted a population of more than 20,000 people. Steamboats from the Mississippi River would come up the Red River through **Caddo Lake** and on up the Big Cypress Bayou to load and unload cargo. It was dubbed the **"Gateway to Texas."** During the Civil War, Jefferson exported cotton from the Southern states. After the Civil War, it served as the jumping off point for many settlers headed further west. The vast timber resources of east Texas went through Jefferson on their way to market.

Jefferson became a river port because of an act of nature: the New Madrid earthquake created a massive log jam on the Red River, known as the **"Great Raft,"** that raised the water levels in Caddo lake and the bayou, allowing steamboat traffic. It is no longer a river port due to an act of man: in 1873, the U.S. Corps of Engineers removed the Great Raft, lowering the water levels. This change, along with the construction of railroads into Texas, led to a rapid decline.

Today, Jefferson is a sleepy little town of 2,500 people. Its gorgeous setting and the efforts of its residents to restore the town as it was in its glory days do attract visitors, however. Many antebellum homes and business establishments have been brought back to their former grandeur. Trolley tours, walking tours, boat rides and even mule-drawn carriage cover the downtown historic district, making tourism the number one economic influence in the area today.

Day 32   Shreveport or Jefferson to Dallas

Distance *From Shreveport: 249 miles; from Jefferson: 177 miles*

Features *This day offers some truly world-class twisties through the piney woods. Visit downtown Jefferson and take note of the old plantation homes on the sides of the roads.*

If you spent your evening in **Shreveport,** gather up all your winnings and get back on I-20 west and take Exit 633 (the second exit after you re-enter Texas) onto Hwy. 134 north after 26 miles. Eleven miles along this road, turn left toward Jefferson in the middle of a 25 mph curve marked with flashing yellow lights. For the next 10 miles, the riding is as good as it gets, traveling over hills and around curves through the forest.

Turn right onto Hwy. 43, go 11 miles and turn left onto Hwy. 134. There are several restored plantation homes along Hwy. 43 to remind you that this was once a cotton-growing region. Fourteen miles on Hwy. 134 will have you in Jefferson.

If you spent your evening in **Jefferson,** take the time to spend the morning exploring this delightful town. Leave town on Hwy. 49 west, ride 5 miles, and turn left onto Hwy. 729 for 23 miles of serpentines through the woods. Don't let the wool gather, as this stretch does have a few curves that will get your "pucker factor" up if you're not paying enough attention.

Turn left onto Hwy. 259, a major four-lane road on which you will travel only 3 miles before turning right onto Hwy. 557. Most of the three miles on Hwy. 259 is elevated and goes over a swamp. After about a half-mile, turn left onto Hwy. 2796, proceed 11 miles, and turn right onto Hwy. 155, which goes off to the left after about 8 miles in the town of Gilmer. Continue on Hwy. 155 for 27 miles of enjoyable motorcycle riding, and then head west on I-20. A quick 100 miles will have you back at your original starting point at the intersection with Loop 635 in Dallas.

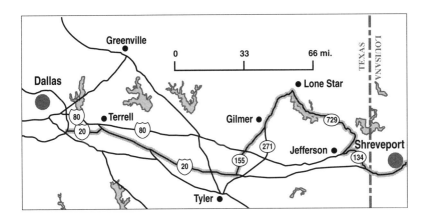

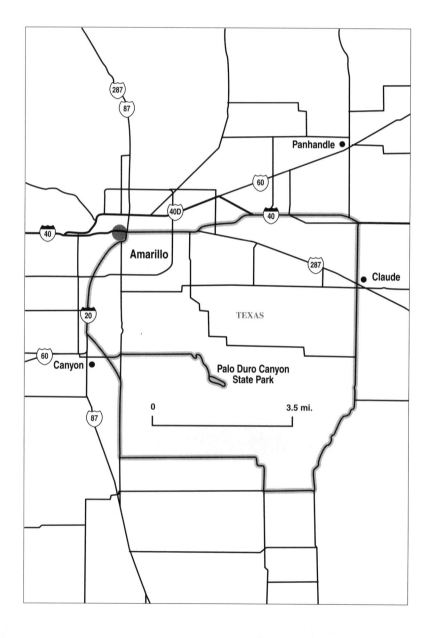

Palo Duro Canyon

If you refer to the overall map of Texas at the beginning of this book, you'll notice that most of the routes I recommend are located in the southern two-thirds of the state. This is because that is where the good riding is. The roads in the northern one-third tend to be flat, straight, and boring. If you enjoy counting telephone poles stretching to the horizon, you'll be in heaven. However, if you are ever on a long trip and find yourself crossing this part of

The Palo Duro Canyon offers a few curves and twisties in the otherwise flat Texas panhandle.

If you're riding across the vast, north Texas plains, the Palo Duro Canyon can be a nice change of pace.

Texas, you'll be glad to know that you can look forward to a nice ride to break the monotony of this stretch.

The **Palo Duro Canyon** is located about twenty-two miles southeast of Amarillo and is quite dramatic. It has a depth of over 1,200 feet from the surrounding plains and is over 120 miles long, making it the **second largest canyon** in the United States, right after the Grand Canyon. Adequate water supplies from springs and the small river that flows through it has given rise to an amazing sight for this area—trees! Historically, the water supply and accompanying vegetation and wildlife attracted several Indian tribes, which the U.S. Army had great trouble locating, since you cannot see the canyon until you are almost standing on its edge. Today it has a state park and offers camping, hiking, jeep tours, horseback riding, and other outdoor activities.

The 120-mile loop that will take you through the canyon can be entered at two locations. If you are traveling on I- 27 south of Amarillo, get off Exit 106 and take Hwy. 217 to the east. From that point, it is eight miles to the **Palo Duro State Park** entrance ($3). After riding hour after hour, maybe even day after day, on straight, flat roads, make sure you remember how to lean your bike as you start your descent. After about 5 miles of a wonderful, twisting plunge on Park Road 5, make a right turn onto Park Road 5 Alternate. This will place you on another curving loop road that is very narrow and should not be taken at high speeds. Just continue onward and you will soon come back to the intersection with Park Road 5; keep straight ahead to exit the canyon.

Although the total distance from the park entrance to the exit is only 15 miles, plan on a minimum of two hours for this loop. The slow speed required, a possible short visit to the visitors' center, and the numerous pull-offs with interpretative plaques and wonderful views make it all a worthy diversion.

When you leave the park, return to I-27. Go south for about 11 miles and take Exit 94. Go east on Hwy. 285 for approximately 27 miles to the T-intersection with Hwy. 207. While this ride is mostly straight and flat, it does contain several 90-degree curves in it.

At the STOP sign in **Wayside,** turn right, continue for about 3 miles, and then make a left turn to continue on Hwy. 285. When you reach Hwy. 207, turn left (north); soon you will begin a fairly dramatic descent into the canyon. It is much wider here than at the state park, and you will have about six miles of good riding into, through, and out of it. Seventeen miles after joining Hwy. 207, you will intersect with I-40. To get back to I-27, simply head west for about 26 miles. Should you be traveling on I-40, take Exit 96 and reverse the directions above.

As noted, there is a lot of good camping in the state park, as well as a small grocery store and café. If you wish to stay near the park and enjoy it at sunset (highly recommended) or sunrise (never been there), there is a good nearby place to stay in **Canyon,** just west of Exit 106 on I-27. For a city of its size, Canyon offers a good selection of motels and eating establishments servicing visitors to the canyon. For a more than adequate evenings lodging, try the **Goodnight Inn** (800-654-7350), located just south of town on Hwy. 87. Brochures in the lobby can point you toward all sorts of day trips into and around the canyon. A personal favorite of mine is the **Cowboy Morning and Evening Tour** (800-658-2613), which features a genuine cow-chip tossing contest.

Motorcycle Transport

If you have limited time available and live far from Texas, consider shipping your motorcycle to your starting city and flying down to pick it up. This will maximize your riding time. A number of brokers have partnered with major U.S. moving companies to specialize in no-fuss motorcycle transport.

If you have Internet access, surf to www.shipvehicles.com. Although this company is primarily an automobile moving company, they also handle motorcycles. Enter your shipping requirements via their website and not only will you get quotes from more than 40 companies, they will advise of the lowest price within 82 hours. Even if you do not ultimately book through them, their site may be useful for comparison-shopping.

Having said all of the above, your motorcycle will probably be picked up and shipped on an Allied Van Lines truck. According to Allied, special discounted rates offered to the companies like the one above could cost less than the prices you will get from contacting Allied directly.

Plan on spending between 15 and 20 cents per mile (as the crow flies) to ship your bike. This expense can be cut quite a bit if you are an AMA member or if you choose cheaper insurance. Allow two weeks for delivery to the mover's terminal at your starting city. You can arrange for the bike to be picked up at your home, your office, or any business location (i.e. your local dealership). Most of the transport companies use special motorcycle-appropriate skids with pads and tie-downs (no crating necessary), all designed to deliver your bike without damage. You will be amazed at how easy and efficient these services make the whole process. For a free estimate and detailed information, call any of the brokers listed below:

Federal/Allied Transport (Rhonda Nagel)
101 National Road
East Peoria, Illinois. 61611
800-747-4100, ext 222
Federal ships close to 800 motorcycles per month and also handled all of the motorcycles for the traveling Guggenheim exhibit, so they have plenty of experience.

Liberty/Allied Transport (Bud Kindermann)
17 Central Avenue
Hauppauge, New York 11788
800-640-4487 ext 1 (pricing information); or ext. 228 (Bud)
Bud is the special American Motorcycle Association representative at
Liberty, and has been extremely helpful to me on a number of occasions.

J.C. Motors/North American Van Lines
1260 Logan Avenue A-6
Costa Mesa, California 92626
714-557-2558 www.jcmotors.com
Brokered by one of the larger California dealers, these guys are shipping
more than 200 motorcycles a month and their rates are very competitive.

Motorcycle Rentals

If you live far from Texas or have limited time, it might make sense just to rent a bike for your adventure. While you lose the familiarity with your own machine and it's associated attachments, you gain the opportunity to try out a different bike without making a purchase. Eagle Rider is a national motorcycle rental company and they allow you to pick up at one location and drop off at another. Note that Cruise America (480-464-7300; www.cruiseamerica.com), while primarily an RV rental company, is slowly adding Honda motorcycles at their 175 rental centers around the nation. It may be worth checking their website to see if they have added any in Texas. Listed below are some local motorcycle rental companies you can contact:

San Antonio

American Motorcycle Rentals
1105 IH 35 North
San Antonio, Texas 78233
210-646-0499
www.alamocityharleydavidson.com
Harley Davidson and Buell rentals

Street Eagle Harley Rentals
903 E. Nakoma Street - Suite 102
San Antonio, Texas 78216
877-931-7433
www.streeteagle.com

Texas Motorcycle Rentals
8902 Broadway
San Antonio, Texas 78217
877-267-2925
www.tmrentals.com

Beaumont

Cowboy Harley-Davidson
1150 Interstate
10 South Beaumont, Texas 77707
www.cowboyharley.com
409-839-4464

El Paso

Barnett Harley-Davidson/Buell
8272 Gateway East
El Paso, Texas 79907
800-736-8173
www.barnettharley.com

Houston

Street Eagle of Houston
12823 Westheimer Road
Houston, Texas 77077
877-679-8200
www.streeteagle.com/houston

Austin

Street Eagle Harley Rentals
5120 Burnet Road
Austin, Texas 78756
877-385-7433
www.streeteagle.com

Dallas

Eagle Rider Dallas
1010 North Loop 12 at Union Bower
Dallas, Texas 75061
972-785-2200
www.eagleriderdallas.com

Additional Resources

There is no shortage of other reference materials regarding travel in Texas. Not so much on motorcycling though. Carry this book in your tankbag as a complete guide to your rides. If you are a true history buff, however, and want to better understand what made Texas what it is today, I suggest you read *Texas* by James Michener; even though it's fiction, it is based on historical fact and can be very enlightening.

Most maps of Texas will be of small use to you, especially for the Hill Country and east Texas rides, because regular road maps can't cover such big areas in the necessary detail. Try the *Texas Atlas & Gazetteer* by Delorme for a closer look at roads and possible alternate rides (available from Whitehorse Press; www.whitehorsepress.com).

Two excellent magazines can be great sources to introduce and familiarize you with the Lone Star State, one of which is written by, and for, motorcyclists; they are: *Ride Texas,* published bi-monthly by Miguel and Val Asensio (512-858-2323); and Texas Highways, published monthly by the Texas Department of Tourism (800-839-4997; www.texashighways.com).

The Texas Department of Tourism does a very good job of promoting the state and will flood you with information if you contact them (800-452-9292; either www.dot.state.tx.us or www.traveltex.com).

Index

A Abbott 97
accomodations 14
Alamagordo 67
Alamo 70–71, 113
  Battle of 19
Alamo Classic Car Museum 102
Alamo Village 113, 128
Alamo, Battle of 20, 71, 170, 174
Alice 167
Allen, John & Augustus 134
Apache Indians 40, 122, 128
Aransas Pass Wildlife Refuge 146
Artesia 64
Asensio, Miguel & Val 219
Austin 69, 81–83, 97

B Balcones Escarpment 69
Bandera 114
Baquillas Canyon 57
Barksdale 125
Beaumont 200
Bee Cave 85
Beeville 168
Benevides 167
Benson, Lloyd 25
Bernhardt, Sarah 141
Big Bend National Park 46, 51, 53, 57
Big Bend Ranch State Park 42
Big Cypress Bayou 207
Big Thicket National Preserve 201–202
Billy the Kid 113
Bishop Oak
  See Lamar Oak
Bishop's Palace 141, 197
Blanco 105
Blanco River 105, 110
Bob Bullock Texas State History Museum 83
Boerne 99
Bowie, Jim 71
Brackettville 113
Brooks, Garth 101
Brownsville 157
Bryan 190
Buffalo Bayou 134
Buffalo soldiers 40, 123
Bush, George H. 25

Bush, George W. 25
Byrne, Bishop Christopher 141

C Caddo Lake 207
Camp Wood 115, 117, 119, 125
Campeachy 139
camping 14
Canyon 213
Canyon City 99
Carlsbad 64
Carlsbad Caverns National Park 62
Caver, Captain Barry 21
Chambers 185
Chisos Basin 47, 49, 53, 56
Chisos Mountains 51
City Slickers 108
Clay, Henry 46
Clay, Henry III 46
Clay, Henry Jr. 46
Clear Lake 138–139, 195
Clements, Bill 25
Cloudcroft 65, 67
College Station 188, 192
Comanche Indians 40, 122, 128
comfort 77, 94
Cooper's Bar-B-Q 88
Copano Bay 147
Coronado, Francisco 19
Corpus Christi 153
Cowboy Artists of America Museum 93
cowboy boots 29
Cowboy Harley-Davidson 200
Crockett 185–186
Crockett, Davy 71
Crossing Guide for Los Dos Laredos 165
Crouch, Hondo 96

D Dallas 178, 180, 182, 208
Davis Mountain State Park 36
Davis Mountains 35, 41
Davis, Jefferson 40
Davy Crockett National Forest 187
Dead Man's Walk 45
Devil's Sinkhole State Natural Area 119
Diddley, Bo 101
dining 15
Dixie Chicks, The 101

Dripping Springs 104
Driscoll 153
Dual-sport riding 53, 80, 88, 202

E Eagle Lake 175
economics
    oil industry 12
economy
    tourism 24, 72
    agriculture 41, 43, 103, 106, 117,
        157, 168, 200
    cattle industry 23, 32
    fishing 149
    high-tech industry 23–24, 82
    military bases 23, 59, 70, 154
    oil industry 23–24, 64, 70,
        135–136, 138, 143, 153–154,
        167, 194
    space industry 23, 138
    tourism 61, 93
Edwards Plateau 117
Eisenhower, Dwight 25
El Camino del Rio
    See River Road
El Paso 29–30, 33, 35, 67
El Paso & Northeastern Railroad 65
Enchanted Rock State Park 87
Evans, Dale 113
Ewing, J.R. 179

F Fannin, Col. James 170
Faver, Milton 42
Folletts Island 143
football
    college rivalries 190
    high school 15
Fort Bliss 27
Fort Clark Springs 129
Fort Davis 35–37, 40–41
Fort Hancock 35
Fort Leaton State Historic Site 42
Fort McKavett 122
Fort Sam Houston 70
Fort Worth 179
Franklin Mountains 29, 33
Franklin Mountains State Park 29
Fredericksburg 77–80, 85, 87, 90,
    92, 96, 98, 105–106, 109–110,
    115
Freeport 144
Frio River 125–126
Fulton Mansion State Historical
    Structure 149

G Gage, Alfred 59
Galveston 136, 139–141, 143, 169,
    196, 198
Galveston Bay 138
Galveston Island 139

Galveston Island State Park 141,
    143, 197
Gardner State Park 125
Garner, John "Cactus Jack" Nance
    113
Garrett, Pat 113
George H. Bush Presidential Library
    191
Goliad 169
Goliad State Park 169, 171
Goliad, Battle of 20, 170
Gonzales 174
Goose Island State Park 147
Goose Trees State Park 147
Gresham, Col. Walter 141
Gruene 101
Guadalupe Mountain 62
Guadalupe National Park 62
Guadalupe River 93, 101, 109

H H.O.G.G. House 200
Harper 106
Hayes, Helen 141
Hays City 104
Hebbronville 167
Heston, Charlton 137
High Island 200
High Plains Drifter 64
Hightower, Jim 25
history 83
    Civil War 32, 40, 122, 128, 140,
        169, 179, 191, 207
    French influence 139, 177
    Spanish influence 19–20, 70, 73,
        103, 139
Hobby Eberly telescope 40
Hot Springs 53
Houston 133–137, 175, 193
Houston, Sam 21–22, 25, 170,
    188–189
Huntsville 187, 189

I Isla Blanca County Park 155

J Jackson, Andrew 189
James River 88
Jasper 202–204
Jefferson 206–208
Jennings, Waylon 96
Johnson City 85
Johnson Creek Park 207
Johnson Ranch 54
Johnson, Lady Bird 100
Johnson, Lyndon 23, 25
Juarez, Mexico 28
Junction 106, 123
Justin, John 180

K Karankawa Indians 139
   Kemah 139
   Kendalia 110
   Kennard 186
   Kennedy, John F. 180
   Kerrville 93, 109
   King Ranch 154
   King, Capt. Richard 154, 167
   Kingsville 154

L La Lomita Mission 158
   Lady Bird Johnson Municipal Park
      79
   Lafitte, Jean 139
   Lajitas 45
   Lake Casa Blanca State Park 161
   Lake Sam Rayburn 203–204
   Lamar Oak 147
   Laredo 160, 162, 166
   LBJ Ranch
      See Lyndon B. Johnson State and
      National Historic Parks
   Leakey 94, 115, 127
   Lewis, Jerry Lee 101
   Limpia River 36, 40
   Logansport 205
   Luckenbach 96, 105
   Lyndon B. Johnson Library and Mu-
      seum 83
   Lyndon B. Johnson Space Center
      138, 196
   Lyndon B. Johnson State and Na-
      tional Historic Parks 85

M Marathon 59
   Marble Falls 80
   Marfa 42, 61
   Marfa Lights 60–61
   Mariscal Mine 53–54
   Martin Dies, Jr. State Park 203
   Mascorro, Skip 7
   Mason 88
   Mathis 168
   Maudlowe 145
   McDonald Observatory
      See University of Texas McDonald
      Observatory
   McLaren, Richard 21
   Medina 94, 117, 130
   Mexican-American War 21–22
   Michener, James 219
   mileage 14
   Mision Nuestra Senora del Espiritu
      Santo de Zuniga 171
   Mision San Antonio de Valero
      See Alamo
   Mission Concepcion 73
   Mission Espada 73

   Mission San Jose 73
   Mission San Juan 73
   Mission Tejas State Historical Park
      185
   Mission Trail 32, 73
   Montgomery 188
   Morgan Steamship Company 149
   motorcycle rallies 16
   motorcycle rentals 216
   motorcycle transport 214
   Mustang Island 152

N Namath, Joe 11
   National Geographic Explorer 35
   Nelson, Willie 96–97, 101, 113
   New Braunsfels 102
   Nimitz, Admiral Chester 78
   North American Free Trade Agree-
      ment 29
   Nuevo Laredo, Mexico 163–164

O O'Keefe, Georgia 181
   Ojinaga, Mexico 43
   Old Tunnel Wildlife Management
      Area 77, 95
   Oliver pecan 106
   Osborne, Ozzie 71
   Oswald, Lee Harvey 180
   Overland Trail 37, 40

P Palacious 145
   Palestine 185
   Palo Duro State Park 212
   Pancho Villa Mototours 7
   Pavlova, Anna 141
   Pedernales Falls State Park 85
   Pendernales River 79, 85
   Pennington 187
   Perot, Ross 25
   Pershing, General Black Jack 27, 45
   Pinion 64
   Pipe Creek 76, 117, 130
   Policarpo Rodriguez 76
   Polly's Chapel 76
   Port Aransas 152
   Port Isabel 155–156
   Port Lavaca 145
   Presidio 42–43, 45
   Presidio La Bahia 171

Q Quayle, Dan 25

R Reagan Wells 126
   Regulators 169
   Ride Texas 219
   Rio Grande River 45, 47, 57, 157,
      159
   Rio Grande Village 54
   River Road 43, 101

road conditions 16
Road Guide to Backcountry Dirt
  Roads of Big Bend National Park
  54
Rockport 147, 149–150
Rocksprings 114–115, 117,
  119–120, 123, 125, 127–130
Roma Los Saenz 158
Roosevelt, Franklin 113
routing 13–14

S Sabine National Forest 204
Sabine River 205
Sacramento Mountains 65
Sam Houston 174
San Antonio 69–70, 72–74, 114,
  116, 131
San Antonio Missions National His-
  toric Park 73
San Antonio River 72
San Elzario Presidio 32
San Jacinto Historical Complex 136
San Jacinto, Battle of 21, 71, 137,
  174, 189
San Marcos 103
San Marcos River 103
San Saba River 122
Sandy 80
Santa Anna, General Antonio Lopez
  20–21, 71, 137, 170, 189
Santa Elena Canyon 47, 54
Santa Gertrudis cattle 154
Santiago Mountains 59
Sattler 101
Seminole Indians 128
Shreveport 206, 208
Skidmore 168
Skyline Drive 40
Smith, Carol 7
Socorro Mission 32
Sonora 121
Sousa, John Phillip 141
South Llano River 107
South Llano River State Park 107
South Padre Island 155
Southfork Ranch 179
Space Center Houston 138, 196
Spindletop 23, 135, 200
Star of Destiny 83
Steinbeck, John 12
Stockdale 173
Strait, George 101
The Streets of Laredo 45
Study Butte 45–46
Surfside Beach 143

T Talley Ranch 54
Tejas Indians 11
Terlingua 46
Texas 219
  history 83
Texas A&M University 154, 188,
  190
Texas Atlas & Gazeteer 69, 219
Texas Forever! 137
Texas Independence Trail 173
Texas Monthly 35
Texas Rangers 21, 191
Texas War of Independence 20, 71,
  137, 169, 171, 174, 189
Tigua Indians 32
Trans Mountain Loop 29
Trinity River 178
Tyler 183

U University of Texas 82–83, 190
University of Texas McDonald Ob-
  servatory 35, 40
USS Lexington 153
USS Texas 138, 195
Uvalde 113

V vegetation 69, 100, 106–107, 110,
  113–114, 156, 201
Vidor 200
Vienna Boys Choir 141
Villa, Pancho 45
Viva Zapata 159

W Wayne, John 113, 128
Wayside 213
weather 15–17, 31, 69
Weed 65
White Sands National Monument 67
Whites City 62
Whitman, Charles 83
Whitman, Narcissa Prentiss 181
Wildlife 51, 54, 63, 77, 83, 88, 95,
  107, 114, 119, 123, 146, 175,
  200–201
Willow City 80
Wimberley 104
Winnie 200
Woods Hollow Mountains 59
World's Fair 72

Y Y.O. Ranch 107–108
Yellow Rose of Texas, The 21, 137
Ysleta del Sur Pueblo 32

Z Zapata 159

About the Author

For the past 35 years, Neal Davis has traveled by motorcycle through more than 21 countries. Many of the adventures of his growing family were on two wheels as well, and he succeeded in infecting them with the "bug." After selling his small business in 1980, Davis took up motorcycle touring with a passion. As a leader for organized motorcycle tour companies in Europe and Mexico, he introduced others to the many motorcycling opportunities that exist around the world.

In 1997, Davis decided to expand upon this attempt by writing books about motorcycle travel. His previous two books, *Motorcycle Journeys Through Northern Mexico* and *Motorcycle Journeys Through Southern Mexico* (available from Whitehorse Press; www.whitehorsepress.com) have induced many to take that next step.

Davis lived and worked in Texas during much of his business career and felt the state, the people, and the wonderful riding available there weren't getting their full measure of appreciation from motorcycle tourers. This book is his effort to correct any misconceptions and introduce the newcomer to the Lone Star State.

Davis' trusty 1993 Honda VFR, approaching nearly 100,000 miles of tender care, resides with him in Boerne, Texas. His dual-sport Suzuki DR 650 stands by in El Paso, awaiting the next sudden urge to get off-road.